WE HC
TRUTHS

A Guide to Wesleyan Beliefs
for the 21st Century

EARLE L. WILSON

WESLEYAN PUBLISHING HOUSE
INDIANAPOLIS, INDIANA

Copyright © 2000 by the Wesleyan Publishing House.

All Rights Reserved.
Published by Wesleyan Publishing House.
Indianapolis, Indiana 46250
Printed in the United States of America
ISBN 0-89827-214-9

To my wife Sylvia
and our children...
Debarah, Stephen and Colleen

ACKNOWLEDGEMENTS

I'd like to thank the many people who have assisted me during the writing of this book.

At the International Center of The Wesleyan Church: Susan A. Lofgren, my administrative assistant, for patiently entering the manuscript in the computer and making necessary changes and additions; Donald Cady, General Publisher of The Wesleyan Church for believing in the project and committing the people and resources of the Wesleyan Publishing House—without his assistance this book would not have been published; Laura Peterson, for guiding the work step by step and providing the editing; and Jim Pardew and Lyn Rayn for providing the cover design and interior layout.

I also want to thank Dr. Philip Bence for his invaluable editorial assistance, encouragement and theological consultation.

TABLE OF
CONTENTS

PREFACE

This is an age of pluralism. Our modern society insists that the rights and opinions, as well as the racial and national characteristics of all people must be blended into such a commonality that individuals are reduced to the least common denominator. To the degree that this fosters appreciation for all persons, regardless of their distinguishing features, this "processing" of modern humanity is positive. To the degree that values, belief systems, social mores, and personal responsibility are lost in indefinable and immeasurable blandness, it is clearly negative. The Church has not been excluded from pluralism. Either deliberately or unwittingly, we Christians have been much less declarative—certainly less bold—and far more conciliatory in our teaching and preaching. The Apostle Paul's personal witness that he would attempt to "be all things to all men" has been carried to an extreme far beyond what he might have ever imagined.

Preaching in the last decade has largely focused on behavioral themes rather than theological definitions. Pastors have done a commendable job in articulating the virtues of right living. We have heard, appropriately, what kind of fathers, mothers, husbands, wives, children, brothers, sisters, friends, citizens, and church members we ought to be. We have learned not only how to worship on Sunday, but how to face Monday with some degree of saneness and sanctity. Self-help sermons abound. Marriage retreats are as common as revivals once were. Consultants serve our every need. There is a "focus" on the family, a program to help men "keep their promises," and retreats where ladies learn how to dress, cook, do their housework, and please their husbands. These worthwhile ministries have provided practical advice, comfort, and confidence to all who are taking their commitment to Christ and His Kingdom seriously.

In this new millennium, however, we must refocus on theological and doctrinal thought. Right behavior must be buttressed by revelation—the "thus says the Lord" of Scripture. That is not to imply that we must discard behavioral preaching and teaching, or question its biblical relevancy. At its best, such teaching is grounded in the Word of God. There are, however, theological concepts—to which we have become strangers—that are foundational to more than behavior. After all, "good works" do not save us. The question of the twenty-first century is not simply, "How then should we live?" We must ask, "What then are we to believe?" This is a call to the Church worldwide to consider again the fundamentals of the faith preserved for us by the Holy Spirit and presented to us through the faithful efforts of devout persons from a wide variety of theological persuasions.

Without apology this book is biased toward Wesleyan thought. I proudly admit that I am Wesleyan both by denominational and theological preference. At the same time, my studies and the experience of nearly forty-four years of ministry have provided me with an appreciation for persons in all theological camps. I even believe that divine truth is so mighty and so awesome that no single theological camp can ever expect to corner the market on truth. It is not my intention to drive a new wedge between the bodies of believers. In some chapters, in fact, I delight in showing the similarities between different Christian belief systems. Even when it is obvious that major differences do exist, hopefully the reader will gain a new appreciation for all believers who sincerely attempt to interpret God's revealed truth and apply it in character and conduct.

John Wesley, the English evangelist who inspired the Methodist and Wesleyan churches, declared that "the mark of a Methodist was not to try to distinguish himself from other Christians, but only from those who were unbelievers." We must all emulate his sense of Christian community: "Is thy heart right as my heart is with thine? I ask no further question. If it be, give me thy hand. For opinions or terms, let us strive together for the faith of the gospel."

This book also reflects recent trends of local congregational life. In my travels throughout the Church I frequently hear, "This is not a typical Wesleyan church." When I inquire why, I am told that this particular congregation has people from varied backgrounds as a part of the fellowship. Baptists, Lutherans, Presbyterians, Assemblies of God, and Roman Catholics might worship in this Wesleyan church. So frequent has been this assertion, that I have concluded that the "typical" Wesleyan church is *not typical*. Obviously, local congregations are ministering to a wide variety of individuals in the context of a community church rather than a denominational church.

Given this important fact of church life today, it will be helpful to discover what distinguishes Wesleyan thought from the views of devout people in other communions. Some of the chapters will approach the subject in that manner. There is obvious harmony in the Body of Christ on some basic truths such as the existence of God, the nature of the Trinity, and the Bible as the Word of God. These chapters will not be comparative in style since I have no desire to compare basic Christian thought with the non-Christian world. There will also emerge on these pages another phenomenon—the variance of views on some doctrines, even within Wesleyanism itself.

It is my hope that I am successful in presenting and explaining theological thought both for those new in their Christian faith and those new to the Wesleyan tradition. It seems important to have more books reflecting Wesleyan-Arminian theological distinctions for those who have not had the privilege of advanced theological education. If in the reader there is created a thirst for more inquiry into the theological thought upon which our faith was first established and continues to be formulated, I will be delighted.

Earle L. Wilson

1

WHY DO WE BELIEVE IN GOD?

A belief in God seems to be part of human nature. People everywhere and in every time believe in some kind of god or gods. Some have highly developed religious systems, while others aren't sure what they believe about God. Many people do not consciously think about God at all; they merely accept beliefs they have inherited or somehow picked up from others. Still others deny that there is any god at all. But for each of these groups, including the atheists, their conscious or unconscious question of God's existence is a key starting point for their thinking about life itself.

Our existence is one of the most basic human concerns and the question of God's existence is inextricably linked to it. Has a child ever asked you, "Where did I come from?" Most children are conscious of themselves long before they ask about God. But it is not long before they explore things such as purpose, value, and ultimate meaning. Which of us has not heard a child ask a profound question which philosophers struggle to answer? When they ask those questions, children are seriously inquiring into the nature of God himself.

In asking why we believe in God, we must realize that belief in God isn't a matter of scientific proof, but of faith and relationship. That does not mean that belief in God is unreasonable, however. Many reasons or arguments for the existence of God have been brought forward over time. One approach states that there must be some truth or principle that is the starting point of all our thinking and enables us to comprehend and explore the world around us. If we believe God is this first principle, He cannot be disproved by the very process that He begins. Pity the poor atheist. He is always arguing against that first principle ingrained within himself and in others. He is always trying to shake something loose that cannot easily be shaken. He wants to believe that all truth can be weighed, counted, or measured. But life isn't that simple. Life does not allow itself to be reduced to laboratory experimentation. Even an atheist accepts as real such things as love, courage, loyalty, and truth. Most admit that God cannot be isolated by and confined to laboratory analysis. But for that reason alone we don't have to reject the possibility of His existence. The fact that God cannot be tested or His existence cannot be proved by scientific method may actually be evidence of how great He is.

Life does not allow itself to be reduced to laboratory experimentation.

When the scientist goes to his laboratory, he goes believing truths about himself and the universe. He believes in the value of reason and truth. Using his reason, he takes whatever he discovers in the laboratory and relates it to his previous knowledge in the search for truth. Nothing stands by itself. Our minds connect all things in a universe of Truth. All people begin their thinking with some statement they cannot prove with their five senses. As Christians, we accept the existence of God himself as one of the foundations of our thinking. We see God Himself as the underlying Reason, the foundational Truth we seek to discover. He then gives us the ability to use reason to discover all other truth.

Another approach to belief in God starts the whole question of His existence from the other end and looks at the created world around us for evidence of the existence of God. Starting from where we are, we find "proof," after the manner of the scientists, for God. The following four "proofs" or arguments for God's existence provide external support for what we have already discovered as the internal evidences in the very workings of our minds. These arguments have been put forward for many centuries, most notably by Thomas Aquinas, a philosopher and theologian of the 1200s. Throughout time, these proofs have been subjected to a great deal of criticism and therefore to considerable refinement in the history of thought. Not everyone will accept each "proof." Indeed one argument may appeal to one generation, while another will appeal to those in a different time. But the very fact that these arguments for God's existence will not go away points to their strength.

You should be aware of these arguments for God because faith is built in part on them. I have determined in this book not to use pretentious words, even though I am tempted occasionally to impress my readers with some. If I promise not to repeat them more than twice, may I be permitted to use a few? I am more concerned with our understanding of these words than I am with our use of them. The names of these four arguments for God's existence are Cosmological, Teleological, Anthropological, and Ontological.

THE COSMOLOGICAL ARGUMENT

Let's take the easiest first—the *cosmological argument* for the existence of God. Immediately you see a word in that name you may recognize, "cosmos" or universe. What's the argument for God? Just this. Take a moment to look at your universe—the sun, stars, moon, earth, trees, mountains, oceans—and then ask a very simple question. "How come?" How did it all get here? Pick up a stone. Look at a bird. Listen to a child laugh. See a leaf fall from a tree. Watch the stars roll by. How come? This argument states that since this universe or "cosmos" exists, some cause must have been equal to the task of bringing it into existence and then keeping it going. This first cause, whatever or whoever it is, must be at least as big as the thing it produced and it also must have the power to produce it. Some of us call this first cause God.

> *Take a moment to look at your universe—the sun, stars, moon, earth, trees, mountains, oceans—and then ask a very simple question. "How come?"*

15

THE TELEOLOGICAL ARGUMENT

Now let's consider the *teleological argument* for God. This argument looks more closely at the universe, sees its intricate and amazing design, and argues that there must be a designer. Look at a leaf. See its structure? Note the little veins. Now think about a seed and how it grows from something so small into something so great, knowing exactly what to become. Look up at the stars and observe the orderliness of the heavens. Everything seems to have design and purpose. Look now at your watch. Does a watch just happen or must there be a watch maker? Look at a 747 jet airliner roll down a runway and take off. Do sheets of metal and rivets and glass just happen to come together and form a 747 jet? Or must someone design 747 jets and put them all together? How long would it have taken ten thousand monkeys hammering on ten thousand typewriters to "just happen" to write the plays of Shakespeare? If you answer that question, remember you would still have to explain the monkeys and the typewriters. If there is design, there must be a designer. And if there is infinite design, there must be an infinite Designer. This leads me quite naturally to the third argument for God. After all, one of the most amazing designs is humankind.

THE ANTHROPOLOGICAL ARGUMENT

We now come to the *anthropological argument*. What cause is equal to the existence of humanity? We are persons and have personality. Could we have come from an impersonal source? We are creative in so many ways. Was the source of our existence uncreative? How do we explain Bach and Beethoven, daVinci and Michelangelo? Are they simply by-products of a process that began when primordial slime accidentally gathered to produce the first living cell? Are we to believe that an accidental, impersonal process resulted in persons like these? This argument suggests that a being infinitely more personal and creative than we must have created us.

THE ONTOLOGICAL ARGUMENT

The *ontological argument* reasons the existence of God from our idea of perfection. Various forms of this argument have appeared, but that of the philosopher Descartes is easiest to grasp. Starting with the idea of perfection resident in a person's mind, Descartes asked where this idea of perfection came from. Certainly it could not have come from a universe that has so many imperfections within it. The idea of perfection could not come from us since few will claim that humankind is perfect. Rather perfection is our ideal. Where did the idea come from then, if not from humankind or the external world? Obviously there must be another source, a perfect one that could implant the idea in our thinking and in our being, and that perfect one we call God.

> *Starting with the idea of perfection resident in a person's mind, Descartes asked where this idea of perfection came from.*

The first reason for believing in God, the argument that God is the beginning of our thinking, is what theologians call *a priori* or deductive reasoning. Men believe something about God as ultimate Truth and Reason and Goodness. The other arguments that first examine the evidence around us and then come to God are called *a posteriori* or inductive reasoning. From examining the universe, we come to God's might. From the design and purpose of the universe, we come to God's intelligence. From the nature of human personality, we come to the personality and creativity of God. And in searching for our ideas of perfection, we are led to the source of perfection in a perfect God. Do we then have final reasons for believing in God? No! But we do have rational reasons for such belief. Putting all the evidence together, it is more difficult not to believe in a God of Truth, Reason, and Goodness—He who is mighty, intelligent, personal, creative, and perfect. One wonders if we really need more than this. Thanks be to God we have even more.

When we search for evidences of God's existence, we discover something terrific. While our questions search for God, our answer—God himself—is searching us out. *"Can a man by searching find out God?"* No, but God comes out to meet us and answer our questions. He does not leave us to search on our own, but reveals himself to us. One way F reveals His power and divinity is through His creation. Psalm 19 says *"The heavens declare the glory of God."* But more importantly, God reveals himself in His Word, the Scripture, and in the living Word, His Son Jesus Christ. We know our friends by their clothing, their walk, their appearance, the sound of their voice, and yet we really never know them beyond their willingness to reveal to us their true nature. In the same way, all our reasoning about God is done in dim light until He gives us His light. We are as John Calvin suggested, like people who see but who need the "divine spectacles" of God's Word before all things are brought into focus.

> *When we search for evidences of God's existence, we discover something terrific. While our questions search for God, our answer— God himself—is searching us out.*

When we turn to the Scriptures, we discover what God has revealed to us about himself through His acts, His will, and His truth. By mighty acts, by holy history, by spoken words, and by His own Son, God has made known His search for us as we search for Him. In Christ Jesus we see and handle the Word of Life. One day, according to the sacred promise, those of us who have believed in Him to the point of committing ourselves to His keeping shall *"be like him, for we shall see him as he is"* (1 John 3:2).

Is it difficult to believe in God? I concede that it may be. But it seems far more difficult to me not to believe in Him. We have never said that faith has no difficulties. What we argue is that unbelief is more difficult.

LIFE RESPONSES

1. Which of the "proofs" of the existence of God suggested by Thomas Aquinas do you find most compelling? Explain.

2. Is it really possible to prove the existence of God rationally? Does one's acceptance of the existence of God depend upon his starting presuppositions?

3. It seems we are incurably religious as human beings. Why do you think this is so?

4. How would you argue with a nonbeliever that the existence of God is more believable than the argument that there is no God?

5. While the natural world forms an argument for the existence of God, how do you explain the inconsistencies in nature which seem to argue that there is no God in control?

2

WHAT IS
GOD LIKE?

Trembling, I stood next to the old man and viewed what was left of his farm. Only hours earlier, a fierce tornado had torn down the barn, destroyed cattle and pigs, moved the house from its foundations and catapulted his car from the front driveway to a field in the distance. "The Lord gave me this farm," he said, trying to be brave through his weeping, "and now the Lord has taken my farm away." I recognized the quotation from the book of Job, but I wondered, did God really take this man's farm away? Is that what God is like?

Another day, after a beautiful Sunday morning service, a lovely couple I judged to be in their forties approached me, hand in hand. They were well-dressed, articulate and gracious. But they asked me an extremely difficult question. "Reverend, our son, seventeen years of age, just recently died of leukemia. Could you tell us why?" I left the church struggling with deep and mixed emotions. Is God the kind of God who does something like that, takes a teenage youth away from his parents for no apparent reason? What *is* God like?

I know God is omnipotent (all powerful), omnipresent (present everywhere all the time), and omniscient (all knowing). I am aware of His holiness, truth, sovereignty, and mightiness. But I want to know, and so do you, what is God really like? A single chapter in a single book cannot begin to embrace the question, but let's at least see if we can discover something of the nature of God which might ultimately help us to understand His relationship to us.

We must first look to the Bible, for it is the most specific revelation of God's character and personality that we have. But there we find God described in two different ways. In one, He is the powerful Creator and seems so holy, so separate, so unreachable. The other way describes God as a loving, intimate father. Can He be distant and close at the same time? I believe both descriptions are true to Him, though in ways we may not completely comprehend. Let's look first at God's holiness and then at His fatherhood.

THE HOLINESS OF GOD

The holiness of God is essential for us to know. When the young priest Isaiah was confronted with the vision of God in the Temple, the seraphim (the angels) were singing, *"Holy, holy, holy, is the Lord of hosts"* (Isaiah 6:3). Notice that they didn't just say the word "holy" once; they repeated it three times. The repetition is a literary device found in Hebrew literature that emphasizes a certain word. Jesus himself employed this device when He used the words *"truly, truly, I say unto you."* The second "truly" was Jesus' way of indicating, "I am about to say something terribly important." In English, we do the same thing by underlining an important phrase or printing it in italics. Sometimes we do both. We don't want the reader to miss the significance of what we are saying.

Repeating something three times raises it to the superlative degree. And only once in Scripture is an attribute of God elevated to the superlative degree—the word *holy* repeated three times. You will not find the Bible saying that God is love, love, love or that God is mercy, mercy, mercy, or justice, justice, justice. The Bible says that He is holy, holy, holy.

In other words, any understanding we have of what God is like must be in the context of His being holy. If we can discover what holy means in reference to God, we may begin to unravel the mystery of what God is like.

Fundamentally, *holy* means separate. Many automatically think that holy means pure, and it does. But that is not the primary meaning of the word. It was not the purity of God that overwhelmed Isaiah; it was the separateness of God that caused him to shake. The theological word for this separateness is *transcendence*. By being transcendent, God is above and beyond us. He is greater than the great, higher than the high, mightier than the mighty. He has power over all and can implement His will in justice, in wrath, or in mercy. And no matter which way He moves, it will always be consistent with His holiness. Even though He came down to us in the person of His Son Jesus Christ, God still remains above and beyond us. The holiness of God is cosmic; it literally fills all time and space.

> *In other words, any understanding we have of what God is like must be in the context of His being holy. If we can discover what holy means in reference to God, we may begin to unravel the mystery of what God is like.*

God's holiness not only describes his separateness but also His character, for the secondary meaning of the word *holy* is purity. God does not have mixed or selfish motives. We see in Matthew, chapter four—where Jesus is tempted by Satan himself but refuses to sin—that God cannot be corrupted. James 3:17 says that the wisdom that comes from heaven is first of all *pure*. Nothing else is pure in itself. It is only as God consecrates a thing that the word *purity* can in any way be applied to it. So then God is holy, that is, He is transcendently pure.

Sometimes God's purity is hard to understand because of His apparent injustice. When tragedy comes, we ask, "How could a good God allow such a thing?" It must be stated categorically that God is never unjust, because He is holy in His justice—He is pure. Frequently I have had people, like the couple who lost their son to leukemia, ask me the question, "Why did God allow that to happen to me or to my loved one?" Perhaps the real question is, "Why does anyone face tragedy at all?" Remember that the universe is in rebellion against God. Remember, too, *"all have sinned, and come short of the glory of God"* (Romans 3:23). All the pain, hurt, and tragedy in our lives is because we each have chosen to sin and to rebel against God. In reality, it would be just if God did *not* rescue us from the consequences and penalty of our sin. If you think you have suffered some injustice at the hand of God, pause for a moment and look at Calvary. It is the greatest expression of God's wrath against sin and His mercy for us. Our sin had to be punished. If it was ignored, God would not be just, or pure, or holy. But in His mercy, He took the punishment for us. If there was ever a being who had a right to complain

> *Calvary is the greatest expression of God's wrath against sin and His mercy for us.*

about injustice, it is God himself. For God the Son, Christ Jesus, is the only truly innocent being ever to be punished. If you are morally outraged as you see what is happening in your rebellious world, let your outrage be directed to Calvary. The Cross will always be the world's greatest injustice, yet Christ Jesus willingly took upon himself the sins of the whole world there, making the greatest injustice the vehicle for our greatest good.

We have never suffered an injustice from the hand of God. It is true we have suffered injustices from the hands of people. But although God may allow others to be unjust to us, that does not mean He is unjust. People and circumstances may mistreat us, and will continue to do so until the universe is redeemed. But since God is holy, He is holy in all His attributes. It is a great comfort that we can trust His justice as well as trust His love. We can rely on the consistency of His character even when He is unleashing His greatest power. God cannot do a foolish thing for He is holy wisdom. He cannot do a cruel thing for He is holy goodness. His power is consistent with His nature and His nature is consistent because He is holy.

THE FATHERHOOD OF GOD

Unfortunately, many people can't get past the distance and separateness of God. Aristotle, the ancient philosopher, concluded that God was the "unmoved mover"—a being that acts in the world but is unaffected or "unmoved" by it. There isn't much comfort in a God like that. Herbert Spencer called God "Eternal Energy," while Aldous Huxley said He was the "Unknown Absolute." An African chief contributed as much as any of these when he said, "We know at night somebody goes among the trees, but we never speak of it." Then Jesus came, and over against these vain attempts to name the Nameless One, He gave us *His* Name. *"When you pray,"* said

Christ, *"say, our Father which art in heaven, hallowed be Thy Name."* And Christ didn't just give us a name for God, but he revealed God as having a relationship and personality that we could identify with—a father.

In the New Testament you will find 275 references to God as Father. In Matthew 6, God is the Father who knows what we need and will feed and clothe us. In Luke 11, He is the Father who gives good gifts to His children. But perhaps the most beautiful picture of God as our Father is described in the parable of the prodigal son in Luke 15. Here is a father who joyously runs to meet the son who has so carelessly rejected him, forgiving his son, and giving him the best of what he has. We know then that over and below and around all the theological terms to describe Him, God is fundamentally a father. For some, this may be a hard identity to accept since none of us have perfect earthly fathers and many have horrible fathers who have abandoned them. But God is a *"father to the fatherless, a defender of widows . . . and sets the lonely in families"* (Psalm 68:5-6). He is the perfect father.

So we have a God who is holy and who is our father and this nature of God impacts our lives entirely. Please do not miss the implications of this fact. Often we divide life into secular and sacred categories. But when Isaiah had the vision of God in the temple, God filled the temple and the *"whole earth"* (Isaiah 6:3). There is no part of the world outside the Lordship of God. Our holy Father is involved in the economic world, the political world, even in athletics and romance.

Didn't the Psalmist touch on this when he says that God is inescapable? *"Where can I go from your Spirit? Where can I flee from your presence? If I go up to the heavens, you are there; if I make my bed in the depths, you are there"* (Psalm 139:7, 8). In other words, there is no place I might hide from God; He penetrates the whole of life. And since He is holy, God penetrates all of life in holiness.

> *We know then that over and below and around all the theological terms to describe Him, God is fundamentally a father.*

We must not make the mistake of picturing God in our own image. We are proud and sinful; we have our moods with our good days and bad days. Meet us one day and we are congenial, but watch out tomorrow! And we tend to think God is like us, sometimes well-disposed, sometimes loving, and at other times like the jealous gods of Greek mythology who grow angry and randomly destroy things. But the crowning glory of God is His holiness. He never acts out of character; there is in Him *"no variableness, neither shadow of turning"* (James 1:17 KJV).

You can trust God, you really can. In a world of partial revelation, still in rebellion against God, we will not have all the answers to all the blinding enigmas of life. But Jesus said that God is our Father, whose very name is holy and whose Kingdom comes to our hearts, our lives, and our universe as we make holy His name.

OTHER ATTRIBUTES OF GOD

My specific purpose has been to establish the fact that God is holy and that His holiness is fundamental to all His attributes. Thus each of us can trust God because of His fundamental perfection. However, a quick review of the other attributes of God might stimulate further thought.

> *In a world of partial revelation, still in rebellion against God, we will not have all the answers to all the blinding enigmas of life.*

UNITY: *"The Lord our God, the Lord is one"* (Deuteronomy 6:4). *"Yet for us there is but one God,"* says the Apostle Paul (1 Corinthians 8:6). The Bible clearly excludes the idea of the existence, anywhere, of more than one Divine nature.

SPIRITUALITY: *"God is Spirit"* (John 4:24). *"Now the Lord is the Spirit"* (2 Corinthians 3:17). On the negative side, this means that God does not consist of the common properties of matter, like solidity, inertia, divisibility, and gravity. On the positive side, He does possess perception, thought, will, power, and action. He is free from all the imperfections of matter and all the infirmities of flesh. He is a self-acting, self-moving, and infinite Mind.

ETERNITY: *"From everlasting to everlasting, you are God"* (Psalm 90:2). *"In the beginning you laid the foundations of the earth, and the heavens are the work of your hands. They will perish, but you remain; they will all wear out like a garment. Like clothing you will change them and they will be discarded. But you remain the same, and your years will never end"* (Psalm 102:25-27). With God, there is no beginning and there will be no end.

OMNIPOTENCE: *"For he spoke, and it came to be; he commanded, and it stood firm"* (Psalm 33:9). *"The heavens declare the glory of God; the skies proclaim the work of his hands"* (Psalm 19:1). God possesses the unlimited power to do whatever is consistent with His nature. This power relates not only to His power to create, but to sustain all things.

OMNIPRESENCE: *"The heavens, even the highest heaven, cannot contain you"* (1 Kings 8:27). There is no part of the universe, no portion of space, in which God is not essentially present.

OMNISCIENCE: *"Known unto God are all His works from the beginning of the world"* (Acts 15:18 KJV). *"O Lord, you have searched me and you know me. You know when I sit and when I rise; you perceive my thoughts from afar. You discern my going out and my lying down; you are familiar with all my ways* (Psalm 139:1-3). Omniscience means boundless knowledge. When it is ascribed to God, it means that not only does He have the power to know everything, but that He actually knows all things, past, present, and future.

IMMUTABILITY: *"But the plans of the Lord stand firm forever, the purposes of his heart through all generations"* (Psalm 33:11). God is unchangeable; He always was, is, and will be the same. He is subject to no change either in His essence or in His attributes. He is *". . . coming down from the Father of the heavenly lights, who does not change like shifting shadows"* (James 1:17).

WISDOM: *"To God belong wisdom and power; counsel and understanding are his"* (Job 12:13). *"God is mighty, but does not despise men; he is mighty, and firm in his purpose"* (Job 36:5). God knows and orders all things for the promotion of His glory and the ultimate good of His creatures.

TRUTH: *"For the word of the Lord is right and true; he is faithful in all he does"* (Psalm 33:4). *"For great is his love toward us, and the faithfulness of the Lord endures forever"* (Psalm 117:2). All God's communications to us are in exact accordance with the real nature of things. There is utmost sincerity in all His declarations and faithfulness in all His promises and purposes.

JUSTICE: *"God 'will give to each person according to what he has done'"* (Romans 2:6). *"It is unthinkable that God would do wrong, that the Almighty would pervert justice"* (Job 34:12). In His justice, God bestows His blessing on what is good, and His displeasure on what is evil.

While holiness refers to the internal disposition of God, justice refers to the display or outward manifestation of this disposition.

GOODNESS: *"Then Moses said, 'Now show me your glory.' And the Lord said, 'I will cause all my goodness to pass in front of you, and I will proclaim my name, the Lord, in your presence'"* (Exodus 33:18-19a). When God's goodness confers happiness without merit, it is called grace; when it sympathizes with the distressed, it is pity; when it supplies the needy, it is bounty; when it bears with offenders, it is patience; and when it pardons the guilty, it is mercy.

These then, are the wonderful characteristics of the God revealed in the Bible that give us a beginning sketch of what God is like. But perhaps the word of the Psalmist is the only fitting way to close this chapter: *"Praise be to the Lord God, the God of Israel, who alone does marvelous deeds. Praise be to His glorious name forever; may the whole earth be filled with His glory. Amen and Amen"* (Psalm 72:18-19).

LIFE RESPONSES

1. Many people divide life into two categories, the sacred and the secular. Is this wise? What is the danger in doing this?

2. What does the word "holy" mean as it relates to God?

3. If God is all-powerful and all-loving, how do you explain the injustices of life?

4. How does the great injustice of Calvary assist us in accepting, with some meaning, the injustices we suffer?

5. Research further the attributes of God to see how they relate to the holiness of God.

3

HOW CAN ONE GOD BE IN THREE PERSONS?

I n His revelation of himself, God has taught us two paradoxical facts about His nature. First, there is just one God, and second, He exists in three persons. References to these two truths are common in Scripture and in the early creeds of the church. The apostle Paul often ended his letters by saying, *"May the grace of the Lord Jesus Christ, and the love of God, and the fellowship of the Holy Spirit be with you all"* (2 Corinthians 13:14). And in the Apostle's Creed, we read that "we believe in God the Father . . . and in Jesus Christ His only Son our Lord . . . and in the Holy Ghost." Such statements have contributed significantly to the development of what we know as the doctrine of the Holy Trinity.

All Christians agree that we have one God—we are monotheists—but also that we know God is three persons—Father, Son, and Holy Spirit. Repeating the creeds and saying the words of Paul's Trinitarian benediction make the idea common enough; the trouble is that we have before us what looks like a logical impasse. Can we really believe that one and more than one can be the same thing at the same time?

WHY DO WE HAVE A DOCTRINE OF THE TRINITY?

This doctrine is not something that ancient churchmen thought up just to make things more difficult for us, although we often think that something is more "religious" if it is more mysterious. When asked to define faith, an English schoolboy replied, "Faith is believing something when you know it isn't so." Many people exercise their faith in that fashion, believing that whatever is said in church is somehow different from ordinary living and can be believed in a different way. They feel that church talk doesn't have to stand up to the realities of life. Of course, such an attitude about our beliefs is quite deadly. We are to walk by faith and to live out what we really believe; therefore, in some measure, we must understand our beliefs as reality and as applicable to life as we live it.

> When asked to define faith, an English schoolboy replied, "Faith is believing something when you know it isn't so."

The Bible declares that there is one God and only one God, and then proceeds to speak of the Father as God, the Son as God, and the Holy Spirit as God. The church has not invented this structure of belief; it has only tried to make statements that are true to the biblical record.

GOD THE FATHER AND GOD THE SON

The experience of God that unfolded in the lives of the first Christian believers was so new and tremendous that it shook their thinking to the very foundations, breaking some old molds and shaping some new ones. The earliest Christians were steeped in the belief of the Jews that there is only one God. They were passionate monotheists, one-God worshippers, and the pagan notion of many gods was a horrible thought to them. But then Jesus of Nazareth came among them. He called them to be His friends and companions. Lived sinless in their presence. Performed miracles before their eyes. Gave them insights into life that they had never received from anyone else. Claimed to have come from a previous existence with God in eternity. Declared He would give His life for their sins. When He died on a cross, His enemies appeared to have disposed of

Him. But then He rose from the dead and resumed His thrilling communications with His disciples.

Now these people were forced to face the question, "What kind of person is this?" They were not about to give up their faith in the God of the Jews, the one sovereign Creator and Lord. And that faith prevented them from seeing Jesus as a second God. What they did was accept and confess a mystery—one that they could not deny or explain. They were compelled to make room in their thinking for an understanding of God that was bigger than they had previously imagined. The Father in heaven is God. Jesus of Nazareth is God. And the two are so related that in Jesus, God actually "comes through," incarnates Himself, and unveils Himself as the God who acts for our salvation. Hence the first Christians confessed, *"You are the Christ, the Son of the living God"* (Matthew 16:16).

GOD THE HOLY SPIRIT

The risen Christ eventually returned to heaven. Then Pentecost came and a sense of God's presence invaded the lives of those early Christians that was so real and so gripping that they knew this was what Jesus had meant when He said that the Holy Spirit would come in a deep dimension of inwardness. This was more than just a kindling of their memories of Jesus; this was the risen Savior given back to them in the personal presence of the Holy Spirit. This too was God.

Now what were they to do with this Holy Spirit? They did not think for one moment of a third God. Instead they were more sure of the Fatherhood of God they had always believed in, and the Saviorhood of the Christ they had so recently come to know. The fact emerges that the early Christians had a Trinitarian Christianity even before they had a Trinitarian theology. Peter, Paul, John, and others were not spinning out a theory. They were interpreting their experience under the

> *They were compelled to make room in their thinking for an understanding of God that was bigger than they had previously imagined. The Father in heaven is God. Jesus of Nazareth is God.*

illumination of God's guiding Spirit and thus developed the conviction of the Trinity: 1) God the Father, for us in love eternally; 2) God the Son, with us in grace historically, but also eternally; and 3) God the Holy Spirit, in us in power—experientially, historically and eternally.

HOW GOD HAS REVEALED HIMSELF

You cannot find a deliberate explanation of the Trinity in the New Testament anymore than you can find a systematic explanation of God in the Old Testament. What you will find is a consistent set of propositions and insights that make abundantly clear the Trinitarian position of the New Testament church.

The Gospel of Matthew records our Lord's instruction: *"Baptizing them in the name of the Father and of the Son and of the Holy Spirit"* (Matthew 28:19). Add to that the record of John's gospel where Jesus says, *"And I will ask the Father, and he will give you another Counselor to be with you forever—the Spirit of truth"* (John 14:16-17a). Then in Acts 10:38, Peter says, *"God anointed Jesus of Nazareth with the Holy Spirit and power."* Add to that the magnificent Trinitarian benediction, *"The grace of the Lord Jesus Christ, and the love of God, and the fellowship of the Holy Spirit be with you all"* (2 Corinthians 13:14). It is never enough to declare that the Triune God has revealed Himself in acts of history, or in the realities of Christian experience; it is necessary to add that He has revealed himself as Father, Son, and Holy Spirit through the biblical writers who have authoritatively recorded and interpreted the saving acts of God in history.

> *Some of the greatest mysteries in nature are merely shadows of the mysteries of God.*

God also reveals himself in the world. Some of the greatest mysteries in nature are merely shadows of the mysteries of God. What we really need to do is take God as the source of all existence and the key to understanding the mysteries of this universe.

Six hundred years before Christ, the big questions were, "What is ultimate reality?" "What is the very basis of life?" Philosophically they were asking, "What is the nature of God?" A number of theories were brought forward. 1) Thales, the Greek philosopher, suggested that reality is water since water exists in the three forms of matter—solid, liquid, and gas—and is part of all living things. Since there is more water in the world than anything else, reality must be water. 2) Another thinker suggested that fire is the ultimate reality because it is both dynamic and static, both being and becoming, two basic characteristics of all reality. 3) Still another thinker suggested a kind of atomic structure of reality, with atoms falling through space and joining together to produce things as they are for a few aeons of time, and then falling apart to join together in other structures as time passes on.

So the problem of the one and the many is common to philosophy—the mystery of matter and energy and physics, the body-mind structure in persons, the powers of the mind in self-examination. These all point to the deeper mysteries of existence, and their apparent paradox mirrors the problem we face in the Trinity. The deep things of life illustrate the deep things of God. The fact that the Trinity—one God in three persons—appears paradoxical is no argument against it. It is the sort of thing we should expect if we look up from the earth toward the reality of God.

THE STRUCTURE OF THE TRINITY

The early church fathers warned us against two things in our understanding of the Trinity. First, we must not divide His essence (we have only one God) and, second, we must not confuse the persons (our God is Triune). Whatever this oneness is, the three persons do not merge. The inner existence of God is characterized by both life and relationship. God is love but love needs an object. Somehow God's love is complete within the life of the Godhead itself.

THE TRINITY AND THE BELIEVER

The doctrine of the Trinity is more than theological lumber; it is more than the reality of the Godhead reflected in the structure of the universe. Understanding the relationships in that Godhead is essential to understanding our own relationship to God. *"I and the Father are one,"* says Christ. *"He who has seen Me has seen the Father"* (John 10:30; 14:9). But we also are in union with God. The apostle Paul says in Galatians 2:20, *"I no longer live but Christ lives in me."* Union with Christ is one of the grand themes of the New Testament. Whatever Paul means by that union, he does not mean that he, Paul, loses his identity; rather he, Paul, is enhanced. The union with Christ is complete, yet in such a wonderful fashion that Paul is more than Paul could possibly have been without that union.

Move to another level of this union. When you read Jesus' prayer in John 17, you are looking in on the unity of the Godhead. His intercession, *"that all of them may be one, Father, just as you are in me and I am in you,"* (v. 21) is incredible but true. We are to be caught up into the very person of God. This is not the Hindu concept of being lost in the All. Rather our fulfillment is in God, but it is still *our* fulfillment that we experience.

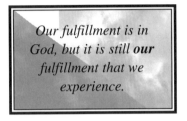

*Our fulfillment is in God, but it is still **our** fulfillment that we experience.*

Paul illustrates this by using the human body. In the human body there is unity in diversity and diversity in unity. A husband and a wife become one, but never a oneness in the sense that he becomes less man and she less woman. On the contrary, their personalities and characteristics are enhanced and fulfilled in that union. There are also unities of friends, of families, of churches, and of believers with their Lord and so with one another. The unities are real and complete, but the persons involved remain individuals. This is precisely what is revealed in the Trinity. The Trinity is the ultimate clue to life, not the ultimate puzzle.

Another analogy is that of the sun in the sky. We see the sun in the heavens; it reveals itself as light on earth; it works in the energies of the heat which we cannot see. So we have just one thing (the sun) located in a given place (as is God the Father in heaven), made known to us visibly (as was Christ when He became human), and energizing us with unseen power (as does the Holy Spirit). This illustration makes clear how one thing is known through another, but the analogy breaks down because the heat of the sun is not fully the sun, as we say that the Spirit of God is fully God.

Still another analogy describes a woman in her three functions as daughter, wife, and mother. She is only one person, but exhibits herself in three different ways or "modes." Her father knows her as his daughter, her husband as his wife, her son as his mother. It is not that she "switches on and off" one aspect or another of her being; she remains herself but is known in three different ways.

In her work *The Mind of the Maker*, Dorothy Sayers uses the analogy of the creative process to illustrate the Trinity. A painter's idea becomes "flesh," and dwells among us on his canvas; that is, his thought is made known in the painting. Then people observe the work of art. Finally, an observer really "sees" the picture, for he is caught up in a singleness of spirit with the creative artist. The observer, touched by the spirit of the artist, sees through the picture to the creative idea itself. In much the same way, the Spirit takes the things of Christ and shows them to us. And when we have seen Christ, we have seen the Father.

Obviously all these analogies fall short in illustrating the mystery of the Trinity. That the Trinity is possible, rational, and believable requires, at last, a leap of faith. The philosopher Immanuel Kant made it clear that there are limitations to our finite minds and that with these limitations, we can contemplate but not completely comprehend things which are infinite. This is not to say that what we know is not true, but that what we know is not complete. My Christian faith assures me that my wonderful relationship with God—where I am one with Him without losing my distinct personality—is possible because this same type of relationship is sustained in the Godhead. And my relationship with God is possible because of *"the grace of the Lord Jesus Christ, the love of God, and the fellowship of the Holy Spirit."* Each member is essential to me.

> *My Christian faith assures me that my wonderful relationship with God—where I am one with Him without losing my distinct personality—is possible because this same type of relationship is sustained in the Godhead.*

My heart needs the grace of Christ. I am bankrupt as I stand before God, but Christ in grace pays the debt for me. He supplies the spiritual capital on which I begin the real business of living. He gives help for the helpless, hope for the hopeless, everything for nothing . . . that is grace.

My heart needs the love of God. I need to know that the gracious act of Christ's dying for me was not just an isolated episode in which a heroic man did His best for me. I need to know that the Cross was the work and pledge of the sovereign God of heaven and earth, a sample of the love that beats forever at the heart of the universe, which is the heart of the Father God.

My heart needs the fellowship of the Holy Spirit. I need to know that this fellowship is the church, God's own creation; it is the fellowship in which the needs of all are the concern of each, and the burdens of each become the care of all. That fellowship of the Spirit produces a wonderful company of Christlike men and women who are the speaking lips, seeing eyes, toiling hands, and marching feet of Christ.

Grace, love, fellowship; Christ, Father, Spirit. My heart needs them all, embraces them all, worships because of them all. Horace Bushnell was a brilliant, restless, and religiously perplexed young man. When he came at last to spiritual assurance through a profound surrender to Christ, he confessed that "when the preacher touches the Trinity and when logic shatters it all to pieces, I am all at the four winds. But I am glad I have a heart as well as a head. My heart wants the Father; my heart wants the Son; my heart wants the Holy Spirit, and one just as much as the other. My heart says the Bible has a Trinity for me and I mean to hold it by my heart."

> Hallelujah, Lord to Thee,
> Father, Son, and Holy Ghost.
> Godhead one and persons three,
> Join we with the heavenly host,
> Singing everlastingly,
> To the blessed Trinity.
>
> —Author unknown

LIFE RESPONSES

1. What has God revealed to us of Himself which we know with certainty?

2. How does the concept of God in pagan religions differ fundamentally from the Christian faith?

3. How does the New Testament approach the teaching that God exists in three persons?

4. Does the doctrine of the Trinity impact our lives as believers? If so, how?

4

IS THE BIBLE REALLY THE WORD OF GOD?

All Christians declare, in one way or another, that the Bible is the Word of God, although not all would express that fundamental belief in the same way. Some believers insist that the written words of the Bible are the very words of God. This means that we have recorded in the Bible, in some sense, the original words spoken by God through His servants, prophets, and apostles. Some Christians would strongly disagree, saying that the specific words of Scripture are of secondary importance. What is really important is the sense or meaning of Scripture. We don't need so much the "words" of God, but the "Word" or purpose of God which comes to us through the medium of the words.

Still others teach that the Bible first conveys the *Living* Word Jesus Christ to us and that we understand the words of the Bible and the Word of the Bible only to the degree that the Living Word is sealed in our hearts. A fourth view is that there is no meaning in the Bible until the Living Word Christ Jesus becomes alive in us through the words; the process of the words taking on life within us and changing us makes the Bible the Word of God.

God wanted to tell us that He loved the world. But we must examine the ways in which He has chosen to say it, if we are to understand. Just as we cannot be true to a composer's music without being faithful to the notes, so we cannot know what it is God is saying, or has said, unless we are faithful to the words He has spoken through the prophets and His Son (Hebrews 1:1, 2).

HOW DOES GOD SPEAK?

By speaking through the words of the prophets, He chose a medium that gave Him both possibilities and limitations. Without question, God was master of the medium for He created the prophets whom he used. The prophets then, even with their own peculiarities of thought and speech, could be properly used by God to communicate what He wanted to say. The original written words show us how God said things through His own chosen prophets. We cannot tamper with those words and still be true to the message. Some versions of the Bible, such as the *King James Version* and the *New International Version,* translate directly from those original words. Others, such as *The Living Bible,* paraphrase the Bible into everyday language rather than strictly adhering to the precise original meanings. While these paraphrased versions are helpful, inspirational and revealing, they should always be balanced by the standard translations. It should be noted that it is impossible to translate anything, even the original manuscripts of Scripture, without coloring the meaning somewhat. Our faith is that God preserves His message so that the translations of the Bible still state all that is necessary for faith and salvation in accordance with God's intended revelation.

> *By speaking through the words of the prophets, He chose a medium that gave Him both possibilities and limitations.*

God also speaks to us through the Word of His Son; in that broken, bloody, beaten, crucified man, God said, "I love you." How could it be said more clearly? The theologian B. B. Warfield used to say that God uses His prophets as an architect uses stained glass in a cathedral. The architect's artistry is in his mastery of the glass to communicate exactly the kind of light he wants. But the glass he chooses may well be bent, uneven, and certainly opaque. Just so, God chose imperfect people to communicate the perfect light, Jesus Christ. This light is the Son of God, the expressed image of God Himself; and in His birth, life, death, and resurrection, we hear, see, and feel the love of God.

When we read and study the Bible, we cannot help but interpret it, much as a conductor of an orchestra interprets his score. But we need the Holy Spirit to guide us, as well as the wisdom of teachers and preachers and our own experience with God. Never this side of eternity can we write "finished" on what God has said through the Scriptures. The Word of God is an endless mine; we will always dig and find more and more of its riches.

> *When we read and study the Bible, we cannot help but interpret it, much as a conductor of an orchestra interprets his score.*

The Word of God was spoken and now it stands written. The Living Word has come in the person of our Lord Christ; we interpret and listen to the Word. All this comes together so that God's Word can speak to our need, bringing strength, assurance, judgment, grace, and the bread and water of life. But in the last analysis, the Word will come alive only as we have been true to the words.

THE INSPIRATION OF THE WORD OF GOD

The Bible is called the Word of God because it is inspired as no other word is. No other writing known to us makes the claim of divine inspiration. Great writers, artists, poets, and musicians are inspired from time to time. But when we speak of the Bible as inspired, we refer to a special inspiration. Isaiah and Jeremiah, Paul and Peter undoubtedly understood something about inspiration in general. But in the Scriptures they make plain that they are writing the very words of God. *"Thus saith the Lord"* prefaces much of the Scripture. None of these inspired writers ever explained this phenomenon to us. But they all claimed it and appear to have known the difference between what they were saying *under* that inspiration and what they were saying *apart* from it. Jesus Christ also claimed inspiration for the Scriptures and for His own words. Perhaps special inspiration cannot be explained. However, the Bible's claims to authority are magnificent and final; our inability to define that inspiration should never lead us to discard its high and unique claims.

Even though we believe that God inspired Scripture, He did not override the person through whom He communicated the message. My seminary professor Dr. Kenneth Maurer used to say, "God prepared both the message and the messenger." Indeed, God was master of His medium as He was of His message. He said "I love you" through the words of Hosea and through the words of John, one in Hebrew and the other in Greek. But like the master artist, He did not have to destroy His medium to use it. God spoke in Hosea's words and John's words and at the same time they said exactly what He wanted to say.

However, the Bible's claims to authority are magnificent and final; our inability to define that inspiration should never lead us to discard its high and unique claims.

The mystery still exists—the mystery of inspiration. How can God speak while a person speaks? Who can understand the interlocking of God and man in the communication of the Word? Some clues to their mystery come to light in the following passages. *"My Father is always at his work to this very day, and I, too, am working"* (John 5:17). *"Work out your own salvation with fear and trembling, for it is God who works in you"* (Philippians 2:12). *"I no longer live, but Christ lives in me"* (Galatians 2:20). Inspiration is part of the central mystery of the Christian faith—God's sovereignty working in such a way that man's responsible action is not destroyed. This is great mystery and great truth. The Bible is God's word in man's words, by God's will in man's freedom.

LIFE RESPONSES

1. Discuss the variety of ways in which Christians describe the Bible as "the Word of God."

2. How important are the "original words" in our attempt to discover what God's message is to us?

3. What does the statement "Christ is the Living Word" mean? What does it mean to you personally?

4. What is the ministry of the Holy Spirit in relation to the Word of God?

5. Christians generally maintain that the Word of God in the Bible is inspired. What does this mean? In what ways is it so?

5

WHAT IS THE NATURE
OF HUMAN NATURE?

*W*hat is man?" the Psalmist wondered. It is a question most of us wonder about at some time. What is the relationship between our bodies and our souls? Should we say "a person is body" or "a person has a body?" The materialist answers that a person is what a person eats; therefore, a person is merely body. But Jesus counters that idea when He says to Satan during His temptation in the wilderness, *"Man does not live on bread alone"* (Matthew 4:4).

We know humanity is unique, despite what the evolutionists say. The differences between humanity and other animals are apparent in the creation chapters of Genesis. First, the whole Trinity participated in the creation of humankind. *"Let US make man,"* said God (Genesis 1:26a). Second, the nature with which we are endowed is special. *"Let us make man in our image, in our likeness"* (Genesis 1:26a). Unlike any other form of life, we have the pattern of the Divine in our structure. Third, the authority given to humans was unique. *"Let them rule over the fish of the sea and the birds of the air, over the livestock, over all the earth, and over all the creatures that move along the ground"* (Genesis 1:26b). Fourth, the way in which we were created was reserved only for humanity. *"And the Lord God formed the man from the dust of the ground and breathed into his nostrils the breath of life"* (Genesis 2:7). These details of our creation are not used to describe the creation of other forms of life.

Now that we know from Genesis that we are created in the image of God, what is this divine image? Theologians usually divide the divine image into two categories: the natural image and the moral image.

THE NATURAL IMAGE

The natural image refers to what distinguishes us from lower forms of created life and makes us human. Fundamentally, this means human personhood. Included in this personhood are reason, thought, freedom, the power of self-determination, and responsibility. Because God created us with these qualities, we are subject to standards by which we will be judged. We humans always live in the realm of the "ought"—the sense that this or that should be done. For animals, choices are amoral (neither right nor wrong), for they are following instincts to eat, survive, or find affection. Humans alone must distinguish between right and wrong. But in doing this, they are acting like God and relating to Him. This responsibility may well be the deepest likeness to God.

> *Humans alone must distinguish between right and wrong. But in doing this, they are acting like God and relating to Him. This responsibility may well be the deepest likeness to God.*

Humans are also given intellectual powers. In Colossians 3:10 we read, *"[you] have put on the new self, which is being renewed in knowledge in the image of its Creator."* People have both natural and moral knowledge and are endowed with freedom of choice.

THE MORAL IMAGE

Holiness best sums up what we mean by moral image, for we are *"created to be like God in true righteousness and holiness"* (Ephesians 4:24). *"This only have I found,"* said Solomon. *"God made man upright"*

(Ecclesiastes 7:29). If the natural image is our personhood, the moral image is our character—the rightness or wrongness of the use of powers given us in our natural image. The moral image gives each person moral ability and makes possible holy character.

By saying that humans are created in the moral image of God, we declare some positive things that will determine our view of the Fall. For example, by being created holy, Adam had a disposition that always responded naturally to the right. Adam was not created in an amoral state. He did not merely have the possibility of holiness, he was holy. If the first person was created in an amoral state, he would have had neither vice nor virtue. Created in the moral image of God, he had virtue but not vice (sin). Adam's first holiness was a holiness of his nature, not a result of his ethical choices. Wesley probably had this in mind when he said, "A person may be righteous before he does what is right, holy in heart before he is holy in life." This was the case of Adam. Holiness was his state of creation.

It is important to clearly identify this fact because failing to do so will make it difficult, in the next chapter, to understand the Fall. Furthermore, it is at least implied in Genesis that Adam's holiness through creation included the presence of the Holy Spirit of God, in his life. Adam enjoyed intimate communion with God his Maker. The Holy Spirit revealed to him a knowledge of God and urged him always to do what was right. The presence of the Spirit of God in man was an original and abiding element in the holiness of man.

Since we are created in the image of God, we come to two important conclusions about humanity. First, a person is like God; second, that person is not identical to God. But the similarity is such that a person can never be seen as merely another animal or just a body. Of course, a person may act like an animal at times. We have all used such figures of speech as "He eats like a pig," or "She is as proud as a peacock," or "He is as stubborn as a mule." Frankly, I suspect such references are not always fair to the animals. But humankind is always, even in our depraved nature, more than animal because we are made in the image of God.

Although God and humankind are not identical, neither are they wholly different, for they are both spiritual and rational beings. But God is always the Creator and people the created. Furthermore, as we will see in later chapters, God is the Redeemer and people the redeemed. This distinction makes more meaningful the biblical imperative, *"Be holy because I, the Lord your God, am holy"* (Leviticus 19:2). Unfortunately, some people read it as, "You shall be *as holy* as the Lord your God." But while we have a kindred moral quality (holiness), we are not God and therefore cannot be as holy as He is, anymore than we can be as wise or powerful as He is.

> *But while we have a kindred moral quality (holiness), we are not God and therefore cannot be as holy as He is, anymore than we can be as wise or powerful as He is.*

Unless we believe that we are both in-breathed by the breath of God, and also made of the dust of the earth, we can never understand what humankind is like. The tension of being both spiritual and physical can be a hard thing to understand. It's easier to think of ourselves as either all spirit or all body. Many people have attempted to make us either one or the other because they don't see how we can be both.

In the last century, this conflict was worked out in the psychology of behaviorism. The theory goes like this. We are merely body and our thoughts are just signals from the body. As the physiologist Pierre Cabanis said, the "brain secretes thoughts as the liver does bile." The result of this thinking was a whole theory of education that affirmed that youth could be rightly conditioned by subjecting them to the proper stimuli. Really, this view says that a person is a robot. Push the right buttons, pull the right wires, and a person's behavior is predictable and controlled. It is rather self-evident that a person is body. But that person is still, even in a depraved state, always more than body. Behaviorism denies the biblical account that we were given life through God's breath and bear His image. And if we are not made in God's image, then we are not accountable to Him.

The second chapter of Genesis clearly reveals the nature of mankind in language not scientific and technical, but simple and universal. Each person is special: both spirit and body at the same time. The body is made out of the dust, the very elements of the earth. At the same time, this physical being houses the Spirit of God himself. Electric current and the wire which conveys it are not the same thing, but you cannot touch the wire without being shocked by its "life." So it is with humankind. You cannot touch a person's body without touching that person, and whenever you touch that person, you find humankind inbreathed and inspired by God.

In addition, we are created in the image of God and need to be in fellowship with Him. So far as we know, other creatures do not depend on that divine fellowship for their fullness of joy in life. There is then a delicate body-spirit relationship, in constant communion with its Maker. Could anyone but God ever have conceived of such an amazing creature?

Now, if you're saying "So what?" let me answer that question. Unless we understand and fully believe what the Scriptures say about the nature of humankind, we will fall into one of two fruitless extremes. On the one hand we buy into the old humanist theory—which the present-day New Age movement has merely dressed in more sophisticated language—that we do not need a redeemer; we are well able ourselves to fashion any kind of salvation needed. Of course, in this school of thought, no one needs salvation from sin since sin is merely a figure of speech, an unpleasant hangover from a pre-Flood age. The hymn of the New Age movement is "Glory to man in the highest."

On the other hand, we end up with the materialist view that humanity is simply another species of animal. We may be a bit better than the animals, but we are made of the same stuff, live by much the same instincts, and die the same death. Nonsense! We are dust, true enough, but we are also a reflection of deity. It is because we are made in the image of God that it becomes possible for God, in Christ, to come in our image. On the basis of that glorious fact, redemption for humanity becomes possible. There are those who hold too high an opinion of human nature and make us gods. There are those who hold too low an opinion and make us not worth redeeming. The Bible rejects both extremes and reveals our humanity as it really is. *"You made him a little lower than the heavenly beings and crowned him with glory and honor"* (Psalm 8:5).

> *There is then a delicate body-spirit relationship, in constant communion with its Maker. Could anyone but God ever have conceived of such an amazing creature?*

LIFE RESPONSES

1. What do we mean by "the moral image of God"?

2. How does the moral image differ from the natural image?

3. Why is the psychology of behaviorism so damaging to the scriptural view of humankind?

4. Read more about the teachings of the New Age movement. How does the scriptural view of human nature contradict such teaching?

6

WHAT DID WE LOSE
IN THE FALL?

The first sin committed by Adam and Eve in Eden was cosmic tragedy. The perfect, beautiful world that God had created was perverted, though not destroyed, by the entrance of rebellion—the Fall of humankind. But what did we lose in the Fall? How are we different now than we were before sin? Any attempt to minimize the Fall fails to account for the evil in the world. But the attempts of some theological systems to maximize the Fall are likewise in error. It is not possible to understand any system of salvation within Christianity unless you understand what that group teaches about the Fall. The patterns of theological expression are so consistent at this point, that once a person has defined the Fall, his theory of salvation is predictable.

The beginning chapters of Genesis describe the creation of the world and provide our understanding of the nature of humankind and human sin. All Christians use these same Scriptures as the basis of their theological systems. How we interpret those Scriptures depends on human factors, prejudice, presuppositions, and historical preference.

In order to better examine the Wesleyan view of the consequences of the Fall, we will first look at some other views.

A ROMAN CATHOLIC VIEW

Many Roman Catholic theologians believe that humankind was created in a pure state of nature. To this pure state God added a supernatural endowment called, interestingly enough, sanctifying grace or original holiness. It is this grace that makes us adopted children of God. In the Fall, our first parents wrecked the edifice of supernatural beauty and harmony that God had built, and returned to their original state of nature. In other words, human nature remained good and intrinsically unimpaired after the Fall; we simply lost that sanctifying grace that keeps us from living a sinful life and destroyed the soul's spiritual control over the body. However, the Bible teaches that sin is the revolt of the total person against God. *"We know that the law is spiritual; but I am unspiritual, sold as a slave to sin. I do not understand what I do. For what I want to do I do not do, but what I hate I do. And if I do what I do not want to do, I agree that the law is good. As it is, it is no longer I myself who do it, but it is sin living in me"* (Romans 7:14-17). This Roman Catholic view of the Fall fails to get the body and the soul of a person together.

> *All Christians use these same Scriptures as the basis of their theological systems. How we interpret those Scriptures depends on human factors, prejudice, presuppositions, and historical preference.*

A CALVINIST VIEW

The Calvinist view, according to John Calvin's *Institutes of the Christian Religion,* corrects the mistake of the traditional Roman Catholic view by properly viewing sin as a revolt of the whole person, body and soul, against God. The pendulum swings away from the tendency of Roman Catholic theology (which restricts the Fall to the loss of the sanctifying grace), only to go to the other extreme and make the effects of the Fall on humankind devastatingly total. *Every* part of mankind is *totally* affected by the Fall until there is no good in humanity at all. There is absolutely nothing to which God could appeal—people are totally depraved or corrupted by sin. Those of us who are not in the Calvinist camp have great respect for Calvinistic theology at this point. We do not forget that Paul said in Romans 7:18, *"I know that nothing good lives in me, that is, in my sinful nature."* The distinction between Calvinism and Wesleyanism is so fine regarding the Fall of man, that more than one theologian will suggest that representing the doctrine of *total depravity* as exclusively Calvinist is a delusion. But we Wesleyans do make a distinction.

THE WESLEYAN VIEW

The typical Wesleyan view of the Fall states that the tragedy of Eden did not leave humanity totally depraved in the sense that there is no good in us, but rather in the sense that every part of us was affected by the Fall. Wesleyans normally do not use the phrase "total depravity" but think of the Fall in terms of "inherited depravity." Inherited depravity suggests that the corruption is not total, as the Calvinist would view it. The Bible does not seem to teach the complete depravity of the total person. Rather, the Wesleyan view means that the image of God is marred, not utterly destroyed.

> *The typical Wesleyan view of the Fall states that the tragedy of Eden did not leave humanity totally depraved in the sense that there is no good in us, but rather in the sense that every part of us was affected by the Fall.*

There are three basic components to the Wesleyan view of the Fall:

1. Sin attacked humanity's essential nature by marring the image of God in us. That image is now beyond self-healing and is hardly recognizable . . . but it still exists.

2. Having yielded to the temptation to *"be like God, knowing good and evil"* (Genesis 3:5b), we now try to run our lives as if they are our own and as if our lives are free from the direction and support of God. That element in us that requires and yearns for fellowship with God is marred.

3. The balance of our nature—dust of the earth, yet God-breathed—is

marred, causing humankind to swing back and forth between life on the brute level and life on the God level. We are no longer what we ought to be and were meant to be. This perversion results in rebellion against our Maker and war within us and against our neighbor. James 4:1 asks, *"What causes fights and quarrels among you? Don't they come from your desires that battle within you?"*

THE STEPS TO SIN

Following the steps of the first temptation as outlined in Genesis gives us a clearer view of the Fall. As we see how our first parents fell, we describe our own temptations and sin. The story of Adam and Eve is the story of each of us; a terribly familiar story. We all were there.

Ten steps are evident in the temptation that led to the Fall of humankind.
1. The tempter spoke and Eve listened. How long the temptation lasted we do not know. Perhaps Eve was strong at first, but under the relentless attack of Satan was finally worn down until she caved in. What an enormous risk Eve took when she decided to converse with evil. Rather than fleeing from temptation, she began discussing sin and what it was likely to do to her. I suppose she was thinking that she wanted to be "mature" about this. If we think ourselves strong, we suspect we can be tolerant and give polite attention to the claims of evil against the will of God. But when we exhibit Eve's same false confidence, we are subjected to the same inherent dangers.

> *But when we exhibit Eve's same false confidence, we are subjected to the same inherent dangers.*

2. The tempter raised a question about the goodness of God. *"Did God really say, 'You must not eat from any tree in the garden'?"* (Genesis 3:1b). The implication is unmistakable. What kind of a God would make such unreasonable demands on you? Why would God keep something from you that is obviously good for you? Once Eve began to question the character of God, she became vulnerable to greater temptation. So would we.

3. Eve followed the tempter's lead, responding that God had forbidden them to eat of the fruit. He had also commanded, *"You must not touch it, or you will die"* (Genesis 3:3). Eve seemed to think that perhaps God was holding something back. She appeared petulant. Immaturity often is. Parents have all withheld something from their children for their immediate good, only to hear them say, "You never let us have anything." In overstating the case, they are inferring that what their parents give and withhold is motivated by something less than the parents' love for them. Eve allowed the tempter this much success. God was under suspicion for putting limits on Paradise.

4. Next the tempter questioned the honesty of God. *"You will not surely die"* he said, directly challenging God's warning (Genesis 3:4). This was indeed a half-truth. Adam and Eve did not die physically when they ate the forbidden fruit. But some wonderful things about their potential and their environment did die, and physical death was now their future. This is one of the truly alarming subtleties of sin . . . its timing. We are able to experiment with sin because there is often no immediate consequence. However, sin must be paid for. At no point does Satan more clearly show himself to be the prince of liars than when he suggests that death is not the payment for sin.

> *This is one of the truly alarming subtleties of sin . . . its timing. We are able to experiment with sin because there is often no immediate consequence.*

5. The tempter appealed to Eve's desire for sophistication by saying, *". . . your eyes will be opened"* (v. 5). Partake of the fruit and you will be in the know. We are not satisfied to know something merely because God told us. We want to know by our own personal experience and judgment. Sophistication is very appealing, especially to young people. We fear we will miss out on something if we don't experiment with sin.

6. Eve made a judgment according to her sophisticated attitude, not according to God's explicit command. It was obvious to her that the fruit was *"good for food . . . pleasant to the eyes . . . desired to make one wise"* (v. 6 KJV). Indeed, this was all true, and all irrelevant. Many things look good in and of themselves. The command,

however, is that we are not to eat. We may, as was Eve, be tempted by seemingly good things, but not be able to anticipate the consequences. Intrinsically, some things may be good, but not when taken in disobedience or when they build a sense of pride in our own wisdom. Many sins go down with the sweetness of honey but leave a bitter aftertaste.

> *We were made for fellowship with God and with each other, but sin separates and destroys that fellowship.*

7. Eve's temptation now led to sin. Temptation and sin are not the same thing, but playing along with temptation already has an element of sin in it. It is not easy to determine when one becomes the other. But once Eve justified eating the fruit in her mind and will, she found no problem in doing it.

8. Having sinned herself, Eve now wanted to share her sin. Misery loves company and so does sin. A popular thought is that if everyone is doing it, then somehow God can't condemn everybody. The suggestion is that we lessen the guilt by sharing it with others. Of course this is a fallacy, but the thought shows the subtlety of sin.

9. Adam and Eve hid from each other and from God. We were made for fellowship with God and with each other, but sin separates and destroys that fellowship. The "nakedness" of this story is not simply "nudity." Our first parents covered their nakedness because for the first time, they could not bear to stand fully revealed to one another. How devastating this has been to the human family. Even the greatest friendship and love never quite solves the problem raised here by sin. Many go through therapy to find acceptance, but the deep problem is sin, for the acceptance we seek was lost at the Fall. Until God, from whom we run, finds us and we find Him, until He restores fellowship with us through Christ, we will never heal these deep hurts.

10. God came seeking Adam and Eve, but they responded by telling Him silly little lies. Dreaming up clever justifications, they shifted the blame from themselves to somebody else, even to God. Now that they had become sophisticated, they wanted to tell God the score. God, however, told them instead that the game of life would now be played outside the garden on a rough playing field and that their opponents would not be restricted from dirty play. The damaging effects of sin were about to kick in.

SIN CREATES A DIVIDED CENTER

Satan's greatest appeal is to our pride. *"And you will be like God,"* he says in Genesis 3:5. Temptation is Satan's suggestion to put ourselves—rather than God—at the center of our own lives, and to make life revolve around us. We know we need God for our existence, and we continue to hope in His grace and salvation, but we want to decide what is good and what is evil. Simply put, we want to run our own lives. When push comes to shove, we will obey self rather than God. We hope to find some way to serve God while we serve the customs and habits of our own community and time. Self reigns instead of God.

When we yield to temptation, we have two centers of operation: the necessary one where God exercises His common care for us, and the impossible one where self tries to run its own life without God. There is no harmony in our being since there is no single core for cohesiveness. With two drivers at the wheel, the machine is literally pulled to pieces. Jesus addressed this fundamental fact when He said, *"You cannot serve both God and Money"* (Luke 16:13c). Or when He said, *"If your eyes are good, your whole body will be full of light"* (Matthew 6:22).

The Fall brought about the disintegration of mankind. Salvation, whether individual or social, brings integration and harmony. This is what Paul undoubtedly has in mind when he says, *"I no longer live, but Christ lives in me* (Galatians 2:20). Being "out of the garden" means that in rebellion against God, we have disharmony without and disintegration within. There is no place in paradise for double-mindedness. Soren Kierkegaard, the Danish philosopher, suggests that to be pure is "to will *one* thing."

> *The Fall brought about the disintegration of mankind. Salvation, whether individual or social, brings integration and harmony.*

WE ALL HAVE SINNED

The rest of the Bible is very clear that what happened to Adam and Eve happened to us all. First Corinthians 15:22 says, *"In Adam all die."*

All people are now "born in sin." Our sin is not confined to sinful acts, but is a sinful condition of which the acts are simply expressions. In fact, the Bible is not as concerned about sins as with sin, the condition of the whole person lost in rebellion and disobedience, the futile attempt to run one's whole life outside of the will of God.

Theologians use two terms to explain what happened in the garden tragedy: *original sin* and *total depravity*. Original sin does not mean there is anything original about sins we may commit. Rather original sin means that our life is sinful in its origins. We come into the world already tainted, discolored, and misdirected. Because of the Fall, human nature is now sinful nature and we all participate in that nature whether we know it or not. Original sin also means that every act of mine has sin in its origins. Apart from God's grace, even my best deeds and thoughts have in them the discoloration of self-centeredness.

Total depravity does not mean that I am totally depraved as you would think of a Hitler or some other madman. The emphasis is on the word "total." That is, the totality of my being is touched with the depravity of sin.

So the doctrine of sin is the teaching that humankind is a fallen race. We are members of that human race and so we participate in that fallen condition. Only through a new birth, a new creation, can a new process be started to restore us to our true and essential humanity, the very image of God. Thanks to God because the perfect obedience of Christ opens this way of regeneration for us.

LIFE RESPONSES

1. Contrast the Roman Catholic, Calvinist, and Wesleyan views of the Fall.

2. Discuss the ten steps outlined in this chapter of Adam and Eve's temptation in the garden. Are there others which should be listed?

3. What aspect of the temptation do you think is the most seductive or subtle? Why?

4. What is the fundamental issue involved in the temptation?

5. How did the Fall result in human beings having two centers of being?

6. What does the term "total depravity" mean to you?

7

HOW DOES GOD
SAVE US?

I f the first chapters of Genesis recount the Fall of humanity from the fellowship of God, then the rest of the Bible tells of God seeking to restore that relationship. In fact, as early as Genesis 3:15, the first hint of Christ's victory over evil is given. *"And I will put enmity between you [Satan] and the woman, and between your offspring and hers; he will crush your head, and you will strike his heel."* Then follows the long, wonderful story of the mighty acts of God working to solve the problem of sin. Having spoken through the Law and the prophets, He came to us at last in His own Son. And it is through the life of Christ—His preparation, incarnation, death, resurrection, ascension and second coming—that we are freed from the consequences of sin and returned to God.

HIS PREPARATION

Our redemption was not an emergency measure or an afterthought with God. It was His plan from the beginning. Jesus Christ was the *"lamb slain from the foundation of the world"* (Revelation 13:8 KJV). It seems apparent, although our finite minds can never be absolutely certain of His infinite thinking, that God wanted us to be creatures of virtue, not creatures of innocence—creatures who could commune with God. The risk then was to give us a choice between right and wrong. This freedom could go terribly wrong, and it did. God, however, anticipated this by having already provided the Lamb or sacrifice to pay for our sin—Christ freely offered and sufficient.

HIS INCARNATION

In the incarnation (in-flesh-ment), God in Christ came as one of us, human, *"born of a woman, born under law"* (Galatians 4:4). At the same time, He was fully God, without sin, the perfect One to make atonement for our human race. Theologians describe Him as one hundred percent God and one hundred percent man—the only two hundred percent person who ever lived. He is Jesus of Nazareth, entirely human; and He is Christ the Anointed One, fully God.

HIS DEATH

The Cross is the central act in our salvation. Christians have been trying to explain what happened on the cross from the day it occurred. We do know that this great transaction on the cross made it possible for God to save us by grace. What happened there to God? What happened there to Christ? What happened there to us? The attempts to answer those questions fill the library shelves of the world. The writer of that great gospel song "The Love of God" stated, "If the sky were of parchment made," the scroll could not possibly contain the whole story.

Theologians describe Christ as one hundred percent God and one hundred percent man— the only two hundred percent person who ever lived.

We do know the Cross provided atonement, which means that separated man can be "at-one" again with God. Paul writes in 2 Corinthians 5:19, *"God was reconciling the world to himself in Christ."* Whatever happened on the cross, God was there; when Christ hung on the cross, the Father was there too. I confess that words break down at this point. The mystery is too great for any vocabulary to handle. But while the mystery is unfathomable, the truth is revealed; when Christ was crucified, God was "in Christ."

Because God is just and holy, the full and infinite price for our redemption must be paid. But we cannot pay it and therefore need a substitute. That substitute is Christ Jesus, who bore our sin and guilt and paid the price with His death. The very One who in His holiness demanded the price, paid the price himself, thus *satisfying* His own demands in both holiness and love.

Christ did for us what we could not do for ourselves. He was "the lamb without blemish," the perfect sacrifice. No one took His life from Him; He laid it down himself because of His love for us. He put himself in our place both to satisfy himself as God and to express that love which would not see us lost. At the foot of the cross we not only see what sin is; we not only see what God in His love has done for sin; but there we are also drawn to respond to that holiness and love exhibited so dramatically. His message now to us is a simple one: "Be reconciled to Me."

How these three aspects of redemption—satisfaction, substitution and reconciliation—play in the process of salvation depends on your presuppositions. The Calvinist, who believes in total depravity—that there is nothing in us to which God could even begin to appeal—outlines the sequence of salvation as follows:

Calvinism
- Regeneration (to be again, or new birth)
- Conversion (to be changed inwardly)
- Repentance (sorrow for sin and wrongdoing)
- Justification (acceptance into God's favor)
- Adoption (reception into the family of God)
- Sanctification (made holy, set apart)

Note that in Calvinist theology, regeneration comes first because the Calvinist holds that we are reborn spiritually by absolute decree and only then turn to God. This is consistent with the Calvinist teaching of special election and predestination. Those heavy words mean that the purpose of God is absolute and unconditional. He appoints the course of nature and directs the course of history down to the minutest detail. His decrees are eternal, unchangeable, and holy. He chooses some for eternal life and He chooses others for eternal damnation. This is His sovereign right and He is as just in limiting His atonement as He is generous in offering atonement for those whom He elected for redemption.

The basic Calvinist beliefs have traditionally been diagrammed using the word "tulip" as an acrostic. What I have diagrammed is "Five Point Calvinism." Many Calvinists would not subscribe to all five, just as there are Wesleyans who would modify the diagram of Wesleyan beliefs I provide later.

> T . . . Total Depravity. Mankind is so defiled that we cannot even respond to God's overtures to us.
> U . . . Universal Election. God's decree by which some are predestined to eternal life and others to eternal death.
> L . . . Limited Atonement. Salvation is only for those whom God has chosen. Christ's saving work is limited to the chosen.
> I . . . Irresistible Grace. The Holy Spirit never fails to bring salvation to those whom God has chosen. God will save all who respond to Him, but only the chosen will respond.
> P . . . Perseverance of the Saints. Believers are eternally secure. Though some believers fall into sin, their sins do not cause them to lose their salvation.

Wesleyanism

The Wesleyan theologian will outline the process of salvation as follows:
- Prevenient grace
- Repentance
- Justification
- Regeneration
- Adoption
- Initial sanctification
- Entire sanctification

Wesleyans believe that God's grace, called *prevenient* or a *preceding grace*, goes before and prepares the soul for the initial state of salvation.

This grace itself is God's gift to sinful humans which makes it possible for us to be addressed by God. Without this preceding grace, the preaching of the gospel would be futile.

The basic Wesleyan belief can be diagrammed with the first five letters of the alphabet.

A . . . Atonement for All. God does not wish the damnation of anyone. Christ died for all whether they accept His offer or not.

B . . . Believers Alone are Chosen. God decreed to save those whom He knew would respond to His offer. He did not determine their response, but He knew who would respond.

C . . . Convicting Grace. This is a prevenient or preventing grace but not an irresistible grace. A person can reject God's free gift of salvation.

D . . . Deliverance from Sin. Believers are freed from the practice of sin. If they do commit a sin, they have an advocate in Christ.

E . . . Endurance of the Believer. The Holy Spirit provides the indwelling power to continue in the grace of God.

HIS RESURRECTION

The Resurrection is Christ's victory over both His and our death. The tragedy of Calvary cried out for God's answer in power. At the close of Mark's gospel, we find women trembling, astonished, frightened into silence. But the young man in the tomb tells them to *"go, tell His disciples and Peter, 'He [Jesus] is going ahead of you into Galilee. There you will see Him, just as He told you.'"* Jesus was alive? The Resurrection makes the gospel of redeeming grace more than the product of overheated imaginations; it was verifiable reality. The revelations in Scripture which speak of our resurrection from the dead and our newness of life are verified by the resurrection of Christ himself.

> *The revelations in Scripture which speak of our resurrection from the dead and our newness of life are verified by the resurrection of Christ himself.*

HIS ASCENSION

The Ascension places Christ at His rightful place, at the right hand of God the Father, where He intercedes for us continually as no one else could possibly do. This is not to say that God is against us and Christ is for us. What it does mean is that Christ, who has done so much for us on the cross, is now standing in the very presence of God; this truth is our intercession. God knows us in and through the finished work of Christ. His presence is a saving word spoken endlessly in our behalf. Life for the believer takes on a different quality when we know that our Redeemer is interceding for us right now. He came as a weak human being, as a prophet-redeemer. Now He is our great High Priest in the presence of God.

HIS SECOND COMING

Christ's return is the final act in our redemption. (This will be addressed at some length in chapter 12). The Bible has not clearly stated the timing or the exact manner of His appearing, but the fact of Christ's return is perfectly plain. As He went away, so He shall return. His coming will bring judgment and new life. The knowledge of His return is a test of our Christian life now. Hopefully our faith is such that we count ourselves among those who would "love His appearing."

So it is. The redemptive story that began with the promise of the "seed of the woman," finds its climax in Christ. God has spoken to us in His Son. Our redemption is not only the mighty act on the cross, it includes all Christ has done in His preparation, incarnation, death, resurrection, ascension, intercession, and second coming. Indeed, He is our Savior from the first to the last. In this He is, as in all things, the Alpha and Omega, the beginning and the end.

LIFE RESPONSES

1. How significant is it that the plan of redemption was not an afterthought with God, but His plan from the beginning?

2. If God knew Adam and Eve would sin, why did He create them in the first place?

3. Contrast the Calvinist and Wesleyan views of salvation. Is there a weakness in either view? What are those weaknesses?

4. What do we mean by the terms *satisfaction* and *substitution* when speaking of the atonement?

5. What is the final feature in God's plan and work of redemption?

6. How would you tell a nonbeliever what he or she must do to be saved?

8

HOW DO WE SHARE IN THE HOLINESS OF GOD?

Various Views of Sanctification

A lmighty God, under whom hearts are open and all desires known and from whom no secret is hidden . . . cleanse now the thoughts of our hearts by the inspiration of the Holy Spirit, that we may perfectly love you and worthily magnify your name." This prayer for holiness from the Anglican Prayer Book expresses the desire of most who seriously study the Bible and seek to do the will of God. But the terms related to holiness often overlap, contradict, and complicate each other until more than one seeker of holiness has concluded that the subject is either too difficult to comprehend or not for him. For example, how does initial sanctification (the cleansing that takes place at salvation) relate to entire sanctification (a subsequent, more complete cleansing)? How does righteousness relate to sanctification? How can we teach a sanctification without confusing it with a perfectionism of some kind? Holiness becomes a doctrine of despair for some and a mystery beyond comprehension to others. The result is the same, a hands-off policy, abandoning sanctification to the people who seem to have an aptitude for holiness.

Bishop Brent, an Anglican priest, came to this interesting conclusion when considering the responsibility of his church to promote holiness.

"It is not merely," he said, "that the world as a whole pursues a course of guilty paganism, but also that the churches which proclaim holiness as their chief program fail to deliver this treasure to their people who truly hunger and thirst after righteousness. If the preacher lays it to the laity that the fault is due to his apathetic reception of the truth, the layman may justly retort that it is rather due to the apathetic, incomplete, and uninspiring presentation of the truth."

This confusion is too often the case. My uncle had been a minister in a major holiness denomination but later joined a church where he was not expected to preach holiness. He felt that sanctification was too complicated, that it only confused people and brought them into bondage. A footnote to that story is that I had the wonderful satisfaction of preaching at a camp in Florida which this uncle attended. After hearing my message on holiness, he sought the blessing of God at this point himself, and received this grace. His ministry-long attitude toward holiness, however, reflects the mind-set of a great many people both within and without the holiness denominations.

The Christian church cannot very well ignore holiness and sanctification (the point or process of becoming holy), however. The Bible is quite explicit when it commands us to *"be holy, because I [God] am holy"* (1 Peter 1:16). But Christians interpret this call to holiness in different ways. To better understand the Wesleyan view of sanctification, it will be helpful to first outline a few of the other theological teachings on this subject.

THE ROMAN CATHOLIC VIEW OF SANCTIFICATION

Remember that the Roman Catholic view of the Fall is that we retained our human nature as God created it, but lost the original holiness that kept our bodies from giving in to sin. Sanctification then, is God giving back that holiness. But Roman Catholic theology at this point becomes dualistic, and fails to bring the body and the soul together in holiness. Thus we may live a rather sinful life according to our nature, but a spiritual life according to our soul. The conflict produced by this dualism is resolved, in some measure, by repeated confessions to the priest who, as Christ's representative, has the authority to forgive. The actual restoration will take place in purgatory where the body will finally be cleansed. Purgatory cleanses the body from venial sins (sins that are not mortal; that is, mere faults), not the soul; this has already taken place. The soul is cleansed by a sanctifying grace ministered to the person through the sacraments of the Church. So a person may be guilty of sinful acts that arise from the sinful body, but the soul of that person is secure through the sacraments of the Roman Catholic Church.

THE CALVINIST VIEW OF SANCTIFICATION

Calvinists believe that in the Fall we became totally depraved to the point that there is no good in us and nothing to which God could make the slightest appeal. Salvation is absolutely by grace. We cannot even cooperate with God in this process. First God must regenerate us, since we cannot respond to His proposal of grace. Once regenerated, we can then repent and confess our sin. Faith follows, then justification, adoption, and sanctification. The emphasis of Calvinism is on what Christ does for us, not in us.

A key word in understanding this distinction is *imputation,* which means "to credit to the account of another." Our sin is imputed, or credited to Christ's account—that is justification. Christ's holiness is imputed or credited to our account—that is sanctification. We are sanctified only in "position" or standing but not in reality. Nothing *in* us truly changes. This is why Calvinists commonly speak of being a sinner and a saint at the same time. We go from being a sinner outside the covering (atonement) of Christ, to being a sinner under the covering (atonement) of Christ.

The emphasis of Calvinism is on what Christ does for us, not in us.

This is a very traditional Calvinist position. A more modern Calvinism picks up John Wesley's emphasis on the Holy Spirit. It states that, while human nature cannot be changed in this life, it can be controlled, not by the person himself, but by the Holy Spirit. So the believer has the choice of yielding himself to his own base nature or to the Holy Spirit. The new

Calvinist winds up with two natures inside. The Holy Spirit wars against the human nature and this lifelong conflict is the badge or the sign of being a Christian.

In this view, human nature is an enemy to be conquered. Every activity and desire of human nature is under suspicion. Every act is tainted by unconscious evil. It would be presumptuous to claim to have a proper motivation. The Holy Spirit sits as a slave master over human nature, suppressing its manifestations and exhibiting its power for Christian service, not by using human nature, but in spite of human nature.

This newer Calvinism speaks a great deal of surrendering to the Holy Spirit and of being possessed by the Holy Spirit. The stress however is not on experiencing surrender, but rather an ongoing attitude of surrender, which may deepen and mature throughout life. It is a life of the Spirit enacted on our property, but it remains somehow external to us.

Both Calvinism and Catholicism follow a Greek concept of human nature that sees the body as the enemy of the spiritual nature and actually imprisoning the spirit. Only death can really bring deliverance. They never quite get the total person together. But Paul in 1 Thessalonians 5:23 prays that *"your whole spirit, soul and body be kept blameless at the coming of our Lord Jesus Christ."* Paul was not suggesting that we are composed of these unrelated elements, but that God's grace brings purity to the entire person. He exalts and dignifies the body as the instrument, not the enemy of the spirit. His emphasis on the sanctity of the body is significant when related to the Greek thought that the body is always evil. Paul's view is also interesting when compared to the Catholic view that the natural body did not suffer from the fall of Adam, and the Calvinist view that the body suffered so drastically in the Fall that the sinful nature cannot be dealt with now, not even by God.

THE KESWICK VIEW OF SANCTIFICATION

The Keswick movement (named after a town in England where great holiness conventions were held) is the holiness movement within Calvinism. Remember Calvinism teaches that God cannot deal fully with the sin nature here and now. When writing about sanctification, the Keswicks play down the references to God destroying our sinful nature, such as Romans 6:6, and instead say that it has been "rendered inoperative."

Basically the Keswick view declares that since the "law of the Spirit of life" (Romans 8:2) is a continual necessity (in the believer), then the "law of sin and death" must not be extinct but simply counteracted.

Commendably, the Keswicks do emphasize consecration and the power of the Holy Spirit in the life of the believer. But their view is schizophrenic, leaving us with two natures—the carnal nature controlled and overpowered by the spiritual nature, but not really cleansed.

Concerned with victorious living, separation from sinful practices, and Christian ethics, the Keswicks emphasize the Holy Spirit's role in the believer's struggle with his own sinful nature. But in their view, the Holy Spirit does not cleanse the heart; as a believer surrenders to the Holy Spirit, he is possessed by the Spirit. The Holy Spirit controls, subdues, and suppresses the expressions of the sinful

> *But in the Keswick view, the Holy Spirit does not cleanse the heart; as a believer surrenders to the Holy Spirit, he is possessed by the Spirit.*

nature. The life of victory begins when Christ conquers and overcomes us. But as with the traditional Calvinist view of sanctification, the Keswicks do not really solve the sin nature problem.

THE PENTECOSTAL VIEWS OF SANCTIFICATION

There is a wide variety of teaching in the Pentecostal movement about sanctification, but three major schools of thought prevail.

The Traditional Pentecostal. The traditional Pentecostal equates holiness with the baptism of the Holy Spirit evidenced by speaking in tongues or unknown languages. While Pentecostalism believes this baptism of the Spirit cleanses us from sin, it doesn't necessarily bring purity, but rather power and the ability to speak in tongues. However, there are just three occasions in the New Testament where reference is made to the "baptism of the Spirit."

1. *"He will baptize you in the Holy Spirit"* (Matthew 3:11, Mark 1:8, Luke 3:16, and John 1:33). This is the word of John the Baptist recorded in each of the gospels.

2. *"For John baptized with water, but in a few days you will be baptized with the Holy Spirit"* (Acts 1:5 and 11:16). This is Christ repeating and confirming John's predictions.
3. *"For we were all baptized by one Spirit into one body"* (1 Corinthians 12:13). Here Paul confirms both John and Christ.

Each of these occasions refers to the baptism in the Holy Spirit at Pentecost. This is confirmed by Christ's saying that it should be *"not many days hence"* (Acts 1:5 KJV). The Corinthian verse also refers back to Pentecost as the only collective baptism for all believers *"into one body."* The baptism in the Spirit at Pentecost was the all-inclusive immersion of the whole church for the whole present age. Neither before nor after Pentecost does the New Testament speak of the baptism in the Holy Spirit as something which happens to separate individuals. The Bible does speak of many fillings by the Spirit as a result of the ongoing effect of that one baptism. But tying holiness to the baptism of the Spirit and viewing the evidence of holiness as speaking in tongues does not seem to have the scriptural support it would need.

Holiness Charismatic. In recent times there has emerged a new charismatic emphasis that has grown out of both Pentecostalism and Wesleyanism. This group teaches, in essence, three works of God's grace in the believer. First is salvation. Second is an experience of sanctification that cleanses and purifies us. This is similar to traditional Wesleyanism explained later. But a third work of the Spirit is added, the baptism "in" or "with" the Spirit as evidenced in speaking in (unknown) tongues.

The attractiveness of this teaching is that it treats more adequately than traditional Pentecostalism the believer's desire for heart cleansing and the means by which God deals with the sin nature.

Catholic Pentecostalism. This development coming out of Roman Catholicism has all the characteristics of the former groups I have outlined, but with an interesting twist. When I lived in eastern Pennsylvania, I would often watch my neighbor sitting in his lawn chair, reading, smoking a cigar, swearing at his children. I prayed for him for months and also that God would provide me the opportunity and the courage to speak with him about spiritual things and inquire about his readiness to meet God. Finally the day came. I asked him if he knew what it meant to have a personal relationship with Christ. His response shocked me. "I'm way beyond that," he said. "I'm a Catholic Pentecostal. I speak in tongues, I visit hospitals and lay my hands on people and some of them are healed. I can speak in tongues this very moment. Do you want to hear me?" All my attempts to bring him to Christ failed because he believed he was far beyond me in things spiritual since he could speak in tongues. I'm not suggesting that my neighbor represents Roman Catholic theology on this subject or that his experience is typical for those within the Catholic charismatic movement. I certainly applaud any measure of spiritual life which has developed in the tradition and formalism of Roman Catholicism. But the fact remains that the emphasis of many Catholic Pentecostals is almost exclusively on the "gifts" of the Spirit, rather than on a life of practical holiness.

> *I speak in tongues, I visit hospitals and lay my hands on people and some of them are healed. I can speak in tongues this very moment. Do you want to hear me?"*

LIFE RESPONSES

1. All Christian denominations teach sanctification. Contrast the Roman Catholic view of sanctification with the other views outlined in this chapter.

2. What do the various views of sanctification have in common?

3. In what primary ways do they differ?

4. Why do you think the subject of sanctification causes so much confusion among believers?

9

HOW DO WE SHARE
IN THE HOLINESS OF GOD?

The Wesleyan View of Sanctification

The Wesleyan view of sanctification basically declares that God can and really does deal with our sinful human nature. We are depraved, true; but not so depraved that we cannot respond to God's love for us or that God cannot save and also sanctify us. He accomplishes real change in people, not just covering up or subduing our sinful nature. These then are the fundamentals which, hopefully, we Wesleyans can subscribe to as consistent with biblical teaching. (1) Sin has a twofold nature—our sinful actions and our sinful nature. (2) God first deals with our sinful actions at salvation. In this sense, all believers are sanctified initially. (3) God also deals with our sin nature in this life through a second work of grace called entire sanctification. (4) There is then a cleansing of the sanctified believer that continues until our physical death. This ongoing exercise of God's grace upon our lives and character is progressive sanctification.

THE TWOFOLD NATURE OF SIN

Holiness and sanctification cannot really be accepted with conviction unless we understand clearly and embrace as scriptural the twofold nature of sin. But the issue of our sin nature has been a hotly contested topic through the years.

Early in the last century, many theologians presented a view of human nature which dismissed any distinction between sin and sins. This theological liberalism denied that the human race had suffered as a result of the fall of our first parents. They taught that each person in turn, faced with the same choice as Adam, makes the same fatal mistake, and that constitutes our sin.

> *Holiness and sanctification cannot really be accepted with conviction unless we understand clearly and embrace as scriptural the twofold nature of sin.*

World War I began to alter our thinking about sin. In the midst of that war, people were saying that "this would be the war to end all wars." We were going to build a new world on the ashes of the old—a world in which there would be no inequality, no war, no unemployment, and no racial discrimination. People were not, at that time, fully prepared to look squarely at the problem of sin, but some theologians had begun shifting their thinking to a more biblical view of the sinful nature of humankind.

Then we were faced with World War II and, at last, the reality of the sin question. How could we deny humankind's sin nature while looking at the Holocaust and slaughter of that war? The pendulum swung almost to the opposite extreme of a hyper-Calvinism. Emil Brunner, a Swiss theologian in the mid 1900s, typified the thinking of the modern theologian when he said, "[How can] conversion [be] the process by which a sinful man is actually transformed into a Christian man? A sinner is not a human being who has sinned a certain number of times; he is a human being who sins whatever he is doing."

Do you see the extremes? Once theologians were telling us that sin is a shallow, insignificant overhang of some evolutionary process which we can handle on our own. Then others said that humankind is actually a demon and sin always remains part of humanity. John Wesley, however, offers a wonderful balance to this problem. He used to ask the following question to get at this issue of original sin. "Is an apple tree an apple tree because it bears apples, or does an apple tree bear apples because it is an apple tree?" The answer of course is that an apple tree bears apples because it is an apple tree.

Now, paraphrasing the question, we may ask, "Is a person a sinner because he commits sins, or does a person sin because he is a sinner?" Is it not obvious that we also sin because we are sinners? So we must always maintain the reality both of the sin we inherit, the sin nature that is ours because we are part of a lost human race, and the sins that we choose to commit as a result of the sin in us.

Will Robinson, one of the great educators of the British Baptist movement, observed, "Men have first to learn that the gospel is not like the advertisements of some patent medicine, creating by suggestion the ills it professes to cure. The redemption from sin deals with a real disease . . . is it a real cure?" That is the question which must be answered by all of us who claim to be Christian. We've seen that sin is real and is twofold. In order to have a real cure both for the sins we commit on our own and the sin we inherited from Adam, there must be a twofold work of sanctification.

INITIAL SANCTIFICATION

God must first deal with our sins. He has done this through Christ whose sacrifice at Calvary holds the possibility of actual salvation for all of us from all sin. So in one sense, all believers are sanctified at salvation. Wesley called this *initial sanctification.* Paul wrote to the Corinthians, *"Adulterers . . . thieves . . . greedy . . . drunkards . . . slanderers . . . that is what some of you were. But you were washed, you were sanctified, you were justified in the name of the Lord Jesus Christ and by the Spirit of our God"* (1 Corinthians 6:11). There was much about the believers in Corinth that came woefully short of even a reasonable standard of holiness, but Paul gives them this . . . *"they were sanctified."* Sanctification always implies a separation, a renouncing of what we know to be contrary to the life we have received in Christ. The evidence of a born-again person is the desire to live a new life on a higher level, to say "no" to sinful practices and a former life style—to separate oneself from all such former sins. So in this sense, all believers are indeed sanctified.

"Is an apple tree an apple tree because it bears apples, or does an apple tree bear apples because it is an apple tree?"

But when Paul prays, as he does in 1 Thessalonians 5:23, that *"the God of peace, sanctify you through and through,"* he is obviously praying that people who have the initial sanctification of salvation will be sanctified—this is the second work of sanctification that deals with our sin nature.

ENTIRE SANCTIFICATION

Could not God have dealt with both our acts of sin and our sin nature in one work of grace? We can't set limits to what the grace of God can do. But normally the newly awakened sinner is not conscious of his sinful nature; rather he is conscious primarily of guilt for sins he's committed. In the book *The Pilgrim's Progress* by John Bunyan, the primary character Christian is carrying around a heavy burden, although everyone else in the City of Destruction is not. The burden, I believe, is not sin itself, but a sense of sin. Christian is a sinner and knows it; his neighbors are sinners but they do not know it. Here is a man with an awakened conscience becoming increasingly aware of this tremendous burden . . . this guilt consciousness that is a result of the Holy Spirit working in his life.

The first concern of all who feel this conviction is to have the burden lifted, to be released from the sense of guilt and to receive God's pardon and forgiveness. If the gospel only offered forgiveness, it would be a gospel worth preaching. It is a wonderful thing to be pardoned, to know we are reconciled to God and are members of His family. And so whatever is taught about entire sanctification as a second work of grace in the believer is not done by underestimating the first. Sanctification is not an ambulance that God has given to rescue us from a weak salvation. The only person who desires a second blessing is the one who enjoys the first to the fullest. We must not minimize the new birth in order to make room for or enhance the doctrine of the second blessing of sanctification.

> *Sanctification is not an ambulance that God has given to rescue us from a weak salvation.*

Others have believed in this second sanctification, but up until the time of John Wesley, the prevalent view was that this transformation could only take place at the time of death. Only in heaven could God effect this profound miracle that would change a person's inner nature. This earlier concept of sanctification was a positional holiness—that Christians are complete in Christ. Being complete in Him did not mean an actual moral and spiritual transformation of the individual, but only that *in Him* are we complete; only in Him are we holy.

Wesleyans do not accept that we must wait until we die to be sanctified or to have the sin nature problem fully dealt with. We believe the arena of our failure is also the arena of our victory. The place where we suffered defeat is the place where God wants us to experience victory over the power of sin.

> *But the essence of the New Testament is that the power of the blood of Christ not only deals with the sins we commit, but with the sin nature.*

The question is, in what sense can God sanctify us wholly? First Thessalonians 5:23 says, *"May God himself, the God of peace, sanctify you through and through. May your whole spirit, soul, and body be kept blameless at the coming of our Lord Jesus Christ."* So God must enable our entire nature to be blameless, which means our sin nature must be cleansed away.

Our sinful nature is somewhat like a blight in a tree or a disease in the human bloodstream. It is a sin infection which is coextensive with our whole mental and moral nature. It is not a separate entity that can just be cut out. The *"sin living in me"* which Paul refers to in Romans 7:17 is not a malignant growth, like a cancer which can be removed from our spiritual nature by divine surgery; it is a moral sclerosis that weakens all the members. It is a fever of the whole body. Who shall deliver us from this? Paul answers for us in 7:24b-25, *"Who will rescue me from this body of death? Thanks be to God—through Jesus Christ our Lord."*

And how does Christ deliver us from the "body of death," our sin nature? By His sacrifice. In the Old Testament, God accepted the sacrifice of animals as a substitute for the sins of the people. In this way they paid for their sins. But there was not provision, in that old covenant, to deal with our sin nature. Therefore, the sacrifice had to be continual. There had to be repeated confession of failure that there might be repeated forgiveness and restoration. But the essence of the New Testament is that the power of the blood of Christ not only deals with the sins we commit, but with the sin nature.

Consider Romans 8:3 at this moment. *"For what the law was powerless to do in that it was weakened by the sinful nature, God did by sending His own Son in the likeness of sinful man to be a sin offering. And so he condemned sin in sinful man, in order that the righteous requirements of the law might be fully met in us, who do not live according to the sinful nature but according to the Spirit."* God not only sees us as holy, He makes us holy. The Old Testament law could not bring an end to the problem of ongoing sin. But what the law could not do, grace can do. What the old covenant could not do, the new covenant can do. What the blood of bulls and goats could not do, the blood of God's Son our Savior can do.

> *No holiness resides in a person apart from the presence of Christ, and there is no holiness which does not issue in love and good works.*

Some in the Wesleyan tradition, however, do believe that our sin nature *is* a separate entity within us, like a bad tooth that needs to be extracted. And once the "tooth" is pulled, then we are completely free from sin. The problem with this view is that it puts too much importance on the moment of entire sanctification and not enough on the process. It incorrectly assumes that we are rescued from even the temptation to sin and ignores the weaknesses and failures of human nature that do remain after sanctification. The place of growth, discipline, process, and the outreach of love as essential to the sanctified life is all but lost. Many who believe in this extraction of the sin nature become more concerned with preserving this sanctification than with serving God. And, unfortunately, this has led to the perfectionism that has given holiness a bad name.

PROGRESSIVE SANCTIFICATION

John Wesley recognized this danger and emphasized the need for a moment-by-moment reliance on the cleansing blood of Christ, a sanctification in which we progressively become more like the perfect image of Christ revealed to us in our experience of salvation and through the Word of God. No holiness resides in a person apart from the presence of Christ, and there is no holiness which does not issue in love and good works. The holiness that is so obsessed with examining one's own holy state that it has no energy left for self-forgetting Christian service is not a real holiness.

Becoming holy, then, declares that the mind itself may be renewed, cleansed, renovated, and made holy. And despite the fall of our first parents, we are both redeemable and remediable because we are human beings created in the image of God.

LIFE RESPONSES

1. Contrast the Calvinist view of sanctification with the Wesleyan.

2. The Wesleyan view of sanctification is based on the twofold nature of sin. What does this mean?

3. Can God actually sanctify a believer before death? In what ways?

4. What is the difference between initial and entire sanctification? Should such a distinction be made?

10

HOW DOES GOD SANCTIFY THE BELIEVER?

Y ou have a new spiritual life if you have been saved by Christ and
this new life of the Spirit brings a transfusion of rich, new, healthy
blood through the entire bloodstream. A vitalizing new life from the Holy
Spirit penetrates your mental, moral and spiritual nature. This liberation
from sin is ours *"because through Christ Jesus the law of the Spirit of life
set me free from the law of sin and death"* (Romans 8:2). The power of
that inner betrayer—our sin nature—which made keeping the moral law
impossible, has been broken. Christ conquered sin so *"that the
righteousness of the law might be fulfilled in us, who walk not after the
flesh, but after the Spirit"* (Romans 8:4 KJV). This walking after the
Spirit is realized holiness. No longer must we wearily struggle to keep the
divine commandments, all the while failing because of our innate
contrariness. We can keep the law with ease because this is the
spontaneous by-product of "walking in the Spirit." To walk in the Spirit
is to live continually under His gentle persuasion, in glad one-mindedness
with Him. This is not so hard as it may seem. Walking is merely taking
one step after another. And with each step of surrender, unholy desires
lose more and more of their power. Deliverance from sin does not come

by continually struggling to subdue the flesh, but by continually allowing the Holy Spirit to fill, renew, and transform our mind.

Sanctification is not the crucifixion of our basic human self; it is not the removal of a sin entity; it is the crucifixion of the condition of self-ism which actually elevates the true self God created within us. It is transition from self-centeredness to Christ-centeredness. That is why I call this "relational" sanctification.

DEFINING HOLINESS

We know that holiness cleanses our sin nature, but what is holiness really?

- Holiness is a restoration to our true selves. It is the true person claimed through and through for God—cleansed, filled, renewed, refined, so that the divine image gleams through our personality.
- Holiness is fulfillment. It is the flowering into lovely completion of all that is truest in our moral being.
- Holiness is purity. The Holy Spirit comes not only to fill us, but to refine all our desires and impulses, to burn away our impurities in the holy flame of His presence.

Sanctification is the experience, originating at the point of completely yielding yourself to God (which is not always a dramatic emotional experience), in which God shares His holiness with us. It is a point of departure—rather than a single fixed point—into a life where fellowship with God and possession of Christ is deeper and fuller than could ever be known otherwise.

Holiness is transition from self-centeredness to Christ-centeredness. That is why I call this "relational" sanctification.

If such an experience of sanctification in Christ as this is taught by Scripture and validated by experience, should not all Christian believers seek this grace? We must each ask ourselves if we have entered that promised life of entire sanctification. Are we living in what Paul called "the full measure of the blessing of Christ?" (Romans 15:29). There is a deeper experience with Christ which the Holy

Spirit wants to make real in us. But we must each go up and possess it by planting our feet in faith upon the clear promises of the Word of God.

I have outlined seven stages which I believe we need to take to appropriate this grace. The sequence of the steps may vary from one person to another, but the issues of each step are quite critical:

1. We must believe that entire sanctification is a gift of God to the believer. If real change is to occur in our moral nature, only God can effect that change. We can only change ourselves superficially. Sanctification is primarily a purifying work of the Holy Spirit in us, a divine gift to be received. We do not earn it, win it, or attain it; we receive it. Sanctification is God's work within you . . . believe it.

> *We must love our Lord so dearly and deeply that we want His holiness for His sake as well as for our own; a holiness that not only answers our longing but brings joy to Him and enables us to better reflect our Lord.*

2. We must be receptive to this grace. If we fulfill the requirement of a loving and complete surrender of ourselves to Christ, God's promise will not fail us because sanctification is God's response to our full surrender to His Son. When you came to Him for forgiveness, you could not see God, but you believed anyhow. Your sense of guilt was acute; you were persuaded of His promise in the Word, and you acted upon that. Likewise, as Hannah Whitall Smith (an early holiness writer) says, "Just as you believed at first that He delivered you from the guilt of sin because He said it, so now believe that He delivers you from the powers of sin because He says it. Let your faith lay hold of a new power in Christ."

3. We must believe that He can and will sanctify us. We must completely cross from self-management to Christ-monopoly. This consecration must be unconditional surrender without a wisp of self-righteousness to it. What we do does not earn sanctification. We must love our Lord so dearly and deeply that we want His holiness for His sake as well as for our own; a holiness that not only answers our longing but brings joy to Him and enables us to better reflect our Lord. Believe that He really does take what we hand over to Him. You will find that it is

easier to receive gifts from an invisible Christ than it is to give yourself to an invisible Christ. But this is what makes faith, faith.

4. We must welcome sanctification as God's will for our lives. There is a tendency in believers to fear the divine will. Maybe we suspect that if we give ourselves totally to Him, His plans will not be pleasant; that somehow He will take advantage of us. In reality, most of our troubles come to us because we are out of the divine will. Remember the will of God is the will of our Father, of our Savior, and of our Comforter. Throw away forever all your doubts about God's will for your well-being. His will is utter love and goodness; welcome it with your heart.

5. We must anticipate sanctification. In God's eyes, you are special whether you are rich, poor, young, old, educated or uneducated. Everything in your present life is part of a brief prelude to a wonderful destiny. Everything here is character preparation for high ministry there. He calls you to a unique and exalted ministry reaching out from your last day on earth throughout eternity. Once He can fully claim you through your own free and loving surrender to Him, He can truly set you apart, sanctify you, cause you to know the abiding Holy Spirit within you, renew you inwardly, enrich your heart, and beautify your character. So anticipate the beyond; all Christians will wish they had been utterly yielded to Christ when they pass from earth to heaven.

6. We must understand what we are asking for in sanctification. You are not asking that God will make you less than human. You are asking (a) that you may be enabled to yield completely to Christ whatever the consequences may be; (b) that the Holy Spirit may fill you and give you the inner confirmation of sanctification; (c) that He may so renew you in the very center of your moral nature, that there is a real release from the bondage of your sin nature; (d) that you might receive by simple faith the fullness of God, whether you immediately feel emotion or not.

7. We must now act and possess this sanctification. Give yourself completely to Christ. Believe that He takes what you give. Leap! Believe! Quit looking inside yourself to see if you have faith. Sanctification is not a matter of your feeling, but of His taking. The very moment you give Him all, you are set apart by Him and for Him.

Now pray a prayer similar to this: "Lord, so far as I know my heart, I am giving You my all, with all my problems, longings, possibilities, and relationships. I therefore believe that You do sanctify me, for I do believe your promise. I trust You now to fill me with the Holy Spirit and bring inner renewal to holiness. I ask You to give me some inward witness to this, deep in my consciousness; but even if that does not come in the way I imagine it, give me a firm faith in Your promise, even apart from feelings."

> *Quit looking inside yourself to see if you have faith. Sanctification is not a matter of your feeling, but of His taking.*

If you have prayed that prayer, accept by faith that God has sanctified you. Let that first step become a walk. Live your surrender daily. You need not keep reenacting your consecration, but keep renewing the sacred covenant you have made with your Lord. Keep trusting that the "witness" of the Spirit is burning within you, and do not allow its seeming absence to deter your faith. Keep trusting that His renewing, sanctifying work is going on within you (for it is) and you will begin to see the change in the way you think and live.

LIFE RESPONSES

1. What is holiness as defined in this chapter? What do you think should be added if anything?

2. Why do believers sometimes fear the divine will?

3. Why is sanctification not a matter of feeling?

4. Has your understanding or perception of sanctification changed as a result of reading these chapters? Why or why not?

11

IF A BELIEVER SINS,
WHAT THEN?

Believers do sin. And how you view sanctification has great importance for what we do with a believer's sin. Calvinists have never had a problem with the fact of a believer's sin, but Wesleyans do. Wesleyans often accuse Calvinists of having a rather anemic salvation when they declare, "we sin in thought, word, and deed every day," Calvinists attribute a sinless perfectionism to Wesleyans who profess that God has cleansed them. The Calvinist hopes in his dying breath to say, "God be merciful to me a sinner," while the Wesleyan boasts that in his dying breath he intends to say with triumph, "My Lord and my God."

Both theological positions impute language to the other which arises in part from a fundamental misunderstanding of one another's view. The Calvinist doctrine of salvation is not nearly as weak as some would suppose and Wesleyan theology does not teach, and has never taught, a sinless perfection. As is often the case, however, the difference is one of semantics. The Wesleyan thinks of sin as a conscious act against what one knows to be right; the Calvinist sees unconscious acts as sin as well. The proper definition of sin probably falls somewhere between the two opposing views. In my judgement, the traditional Wesleyan notion of what constitutes sin is simply too limited, while the Calvinist tends to go too far the other way by including faults and human frailties in the definition of sin. We should not suggest that our humanness is somehow sinful; at the same time, the more eager we are to be like Christ, the more we are aware of sin in our lives.

WE ARE SAVED FROM THE PRACTICE OF SIN

It is a magnificent thing to be saved. The Bible declares that *"if anyone is in Christ, he is a new creation; the old has gone, the new has come"* (2 Corinthians 5:17). Wesleyans believe, along with many other Christian groups, "that regeneration, or the new birth, is that work of the Holy Spirit whereby, when one truly repents and believes, one's moral nature is given a distinctively spiritual life with the capacity for love and obedience. This new life is received by faith in Jesus Christ, it enables the pardoned sinner to serve God with the will and affections of the heart, and by it the regenerate are delivered from the power of sin which reigns over all the unregenerate (1996 Discipline of The Wesleyan Church, Paragraph 230).

A person converted to Christ Jesus begins a new life which includes turning from the old life with its sinful practices. The Apostle Paul described this conversion as life-transforming time and again. To the Thessalonians, for example, he declared that *"you turned to God from idols to serve the living and true God"* (1 Thessalonians 1:9).

> We should not suggest that our humanness is somehow sinful; at the same time, the more eager we are to be like Christ, the more we are aware of sin in our lives.

First John 3 makes quite clear the teaching that a child of God no longer continues the practice of sinning. *"No one who lives in Him keeps on sinning. No one who continues to sin has either seen Him or known Him. . . .No one who is born of God will continue to sin, because God's seed remains in Him; he cannot go on sinning, because he has been born of God"* (vv. 6, 9). A life of continual sinning is simply incompatible with the new life we have received from Christ. Against the tendency of this present culture to excuse sinful behavior, or to blame others for our moral failures, the clear New Testament command to live a consistent righteous life is refreshing. The Calvinist suggestion that one is both a Christian and a sinner at the same time is extremely difficult for Wesleyans to accept. Conversion to Christ must be more than an experiential bump on the road of a life of sinning. Our life after being forgiven and saved by Christ certainly must be markedly different from our life before knowing Him. Salvation not only provides eternal life but a new quality of life here and now.

> *Conversion to Christ must be more than an experiential bump on the road of a life of sinning. Our life after being forgiven and saved by Christ certainly must be markedly different from our life before knowing Him.*

THE BELIEVER CAN AND MAY INDEED SIN

At the same time, John is obviously writing to believers when he says, *"My dear children, I write this to you so that you will not sin. But if anybody does sin, we have one who speaks to the Father in our defense— Jesus Christ, the Righteous One. He is the atoning sacrifice for our sins, and not only for ours but also for the sins of the whole world"* (1 John 2:1, 2). The believer does not make a practice of sinning, but if the believer never sins, why would there be an "Advocate" for the believer? Obviously we never reach the point in this life where we are beyond being vulnerable to temptation. The simple but uncomfortable fact is that until we reach heaven, there exists the possibility of us being *"caught in sin"* (Galatians 6:1). Not only is there a possibility, but for most of us, there is the likelihood that we will sin.

At times, our definition of sin is far too limited. We describe sin exclusively in terms of sexual sins or inappropriate physical acts, and ignore the sins of the spirit—anger, jealousy, resentment, negativism, pride, self-centeredness. As we mature in the Christian life, we begin to realize the dimensions of the Fall reflected in each of us. Our potential for sin goes far beyond the narrow dimensions we once thought and embraces our motives, attitudes, prejudices, and even the secrets of our heart and mind. We are forced to ask the question, "How do I as a believer respond to my sin?"

> *There should be no spiritual pride in any of us when we minister to a person who has sinned— no hint of superiority, no contempt for the one who has fallen, no forgetfulness that we all face temptation.*

The Bible clearly teaches how to handle others who may have been overtaken in a sin. Paul says *"If someone is caught in a sin, you who are spiritual should restore him gently. But watch yourself, or you also may be tempted"* (Galatians 6:1). There should be no spiritual pride in any of us when we minister to a person who has sinned—no hint of superiority, no contempt for the one who has fallen, no forgetfulness that we all face temptation. Rather in love, tenderness, and spiritual sensitivity, we do what we can to bring that person to a confession of the sin and an acceptance of God's forgiveness.

This gentle rebuke Paul mentions is part of the ministry of every local congregation. Our churches must assume the difficult task of bringing a Bible-centered, Holy Spirit-sensitive, Christ-honoring, and wise and impartial discipline to bear upon its members. The Apostle Paul criticized the church in Corinth because it failed to deal appropriately with a member guilty of a sexual sin. In his second letter to Corinth, he commended them for finally fulfilling that ministry. The strong desire to retain everyone who attends, along with the tendency of people to move from one church to another rather than face impending discipline, contributes to the lack of congregational discipline today.

Some Christians deny the right of a church to discipline it members, but God gives this power to every scriptural Church. Even secular clubs deal with offending members, either by censoring them or removing them from membership. All true Christians have separated themselves from the world and have placed themselves under the laws of Christ. They maintain a special relationship with Him so long as they are faithful. They are the objects of His care and love, as members of His own body, and to them great promises are made. To preserve them in this state of fidelity, to guard them from errors in doctrine and the practice of sin, and thus to prevent their separation from Christ, the Church was established. The failure of our churches to exercise this authority over members who err might result in retaining that member in the local body, but risk their expulsion from Christ's universal Church. We will minister most effectively to all, particularly to the one who is *"caught in sin,"* if we diligently maintain a proper perspective and balance between our duties and our rights in the local congregation.

An even larger issue for most if us is "How do you handle yourself when you sin?" Most, if not all, Christians stumble in one way or another. Jesus Himself said, *"When you pray, say . . . forgive us our sins, for we also forgive everyone who sins against us"* (Luke 11:4) Christ would not have encouraged a prayer His disciples would not need.

There are a number of directions we could go in response to our sin. 1) We may be tempted to simply go on in the sin, denying that it is sin at all. 2) We may make restitution and believe, falsely, that restitution, as important as it is, has cancelled out the sin. 3) Or we may be so engulfed in the shame of our sin that we just give up altogether. All such courses fail miserably in bringing us to the repentance required and the forgiveness accepted.

DO NOT MINIMIZE THE SIN

We should never let ourselves off lightly; never suggest in any way that the sin, whatever it was, is not important. To excuse ourselves of any sin is to bring judgment upon ourselves. The Bible makes it quite clear that there are eternal consequences for sin: *"The wages of sin is death"* (Romans 6:23). As we instinctively seek to protect our bodies from danger, so we should find ways to protect ourselves from guilt.

There are at least three possible responses when we are faced with the guilt associated with sin. We may tamper with the labels; that is, call a sin something less than it is. By giving the sin a less offensive name, we attempt to sneak the guilt past our moral guard. We actually began this practice in childhood. When our parents accused us of lying, we called it a fib. Even adults find comfort in distinguishing between white lies and

> *We should never let ourselves off lightly; never suggest in any way that the sin, whatever it was, is not important.*

black lies, as though the white ones were not really lies. Modern sophistication uses terms like premarital sex or extramarital affairs; of course the Bible calls this fornication and adultery. New labels for old evils—a minimizing of sin. I'm reminded of the old rhyme I learned many years ago:

> In olden days when people heard a swindler huge had come to grief,
> They used a good old Saxon word, and called the man a 'thief.'
> But language such as that today upon our tender feelings grates,
> Now they look wise and simply say, "he re-hypothecates."
> (I'm not sure what it means either)

When the prodigal son from Jesus' parable in Luke 15 left home, he called it "independence"; when he was in the far country, he called it "pleasure"; when he ran into difficulty and lost his inheritance, he called it "bad luck"; but when he finally came to himself, he said, "I have sinned." And that is when he found forgiveness and restoration.

This is the first trap to avoid: never minimize the sinfulness of sin. You cannot make a deadly thing friendly by employing a light name. Cancer is cancer even when you call it indigestion. I suggest, when I counsel people, that they use the same term to describe their own sin that they would employ if someone else did the same thing. Whatever term you would use to describe someone else's trespass, use to describe your own and you will be on the way to repentance.

> *By giving the sin a less offensive name, we attempt to sneak the guilt past our moral guard.*

The second trap to avoid is deceiving yourself into believing that sin is ever justified by circumstances. How did you get into that guilty relationship? "I was lonely," you respond. But aren't other people lonely? And cannot God deliver us from sin in spite of our loneliness? How did you come to pass on that slander? "Somebody told me," is your answer. But don't people often tell you half-truths? Did you first inquire whether it had any foundation in fact? Or were you just anxious to pass it on? Could it be that jealousy led you to speak? No, don't ever excuse yourself on the ground of circumstances. Admit the sin. Own up to it. There is nothing quite so healthy, nothing so spiritually healing as dropping all evasions and admitting fault.

The third trap to avoid is attempting to persuade oneself that morality varies from one generation to another. We are dealing with the laws of an eternal God. When God gave the Ten Commandments, He did not give them only to a few Jewish tribes. He gave them to the Israelites so that they might become laws for all humanity for all time. They were meant to be the basis of all morality. Time makes no difference to the moral counsels of God; neither does one's station in life. Customs may change and do, but not the decrees of God.

> *There is nothing quite so healthy, nothing so spiritually healing as dropping all evasions and admitting fault.*

God's moral law is not subject to popular polls or personal opinion. Neither science nor sophistication can alter what God has declared. God's law is like middle C on a piano. You can measure your life and soul from it. If you observe and avoid these traps, you will see sin for the loathsome thing it is, turn from it, and find the forgiveness offered in Christ.

DO NOT MAXIMIZE THE SIN

Conscientious believers usually do not minimize their sins, but rather maximize them. And how do we do that? By failing to forgive ourselves after we have accepted the forgiveness of God. I am convinced that this is a fatal flaw in the life of many believers. We do not doubt God's forgiveness; we just never seem quite able to forgive ourselves. The memory of the trespass lacerates us and we cannot get it out of our minds. Just like an unhealed wound in the body, an unhealed wound in the spirit drains our strength, hinders our progress, pours poison into our spiritual bloodstream, and makes us invalids. In over forty years of ministry, I have encountered more people who fall into this error than any other. In wanting to demonstrate to God their deep sorrow for their sin and their level of contrition, they fail to forgive themselves.

We should forgive ourselves after receiving the forgiveness of God for two fundamental reasons. Our unwillingness to forgive ourselves is a form of spiritual pride. When we do not forgive ourselves, we are really saying, "How could I have done that? I have had so many spiritual advantages and been trained in the Word of God. How I hate myself." Notice the attention to "I". This self-hate does not aid repentance, it destroys us. This exaggerated attempt at humility is really inverted pride. You are actually lifting yourself above the very holiness of God and saying, "God, you might be able to forgive me of this sin, but if Your standard of holiness was as high as my standard, You would not be so quick to forgive it."

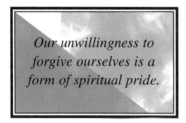

Our unwillingness to forgive ourselves is a form of spiritual pride.

Accept the forgiveness of God by forgiving yourself. You cannot undo the past, but if God has forgiven you (and He has if you have truly repented), then who can justly condemn you? No one, not even yourself. All of our sins, confessed to God, are buried in the sea of His forgetfulness. Satan may bring them to our memory, but if God forgives them, who are we not to forgive ourselves?

There is a second reason why we must forgive ourselves once God has done so. In a mysterious way that goes beyond human fathoming, God has a way of using even sin and failure in a positive way. Obviously, God does not tolerate sin; but the same God who is mighty in creation is great in transformation. He can take the very evil that destroys and turn it to redemptive purposes. The greatest illustration of that, of course, is the Cross itself. Putting Christ on the cross was the foulest thing our race ever did; but it became the most sublime thing God ever used. The Cross was humanity's worst, but at the same time it was heaven's best; our depth, but God's zenith. If God is able to do that with the Cross, can He not do something similar with your worst?

Take your sin to God, and He will make something positive out of it. He will not encourage you to talk about it, but He will use it to help drive the engines of your will. He will quicken your compassion for other sinners and make you more sensitive to the fallen when other Christians give the impression that God is hard and unforgiving.

Saul, who became Paul the Apostle, once held the coats of those who stoned the first martyr, Stephen, to death. This same Paul led the charge against the early church by persecuting and imprisoning the early

Christians. Having been forgiven by God of such sins, Paul forgave himself. In forgiving himself he found that God used his memory of his former life of sin as the force to drive him to serve the Lord and His Church even through many hardships. Paul could have condemned himself and never have been used by God. But God turned this great persecutor into the greatest of all proclaimers. God can certainly do the same for you.

It is Satan's wish to cripple our lives; God in His grace, restores us to our new life in Him. Recognizing God's ability to do that should inspire us to not allow the past to paralyze us, and to move with confidence to our future in service to Him and His Church.

CLAIM THE FULL MEASURE OF GOD'S GRACE

While we can never reach a point here where sinning is beyond the realm of possibility, many believers are stumbling too often—having too many spiritual flat tires—because they are attempting to live the Christian life in their own strength rather than in the power of the Spirit of God. Although Calvinists insist that we sin in thought, word, and deed every day, Wesleyans, while guarding against perfectionism, assert that by living in the Spirit we can and must live a consistent Christian life. We may sin at times, but such failure should become less and less frequent.

Our spiritual fathers had a simple technique they employed for convincing people that habitual sinning isn't necessary. They would ask, "Can you live without sin for a minute?" The answer would be, "Yes." "How about two minutes? Five minutes? An hour?" You can readily see how their simple logic worked. They did not argue that anyone but our Lord ever lived without sin; they just insisted that sin in a redeemed person isn't necessary. Charles Wesley's hymns have captured the passion of our fathers.

> *While we can never reach a point here where sinning is beyond the realm of possibility, many believers are stumbling too often—having too many spiritual flat tires.*

He wills that I should holy be,
That holiness I long to feel,
That full Divine conformity
To all my Savior's righteous will.

Charles Wesley also sang about the miracles of the Christian life—
the things which never could be, it seemed, and yet which God would
sometimes bring to pass.

The most impossible of all
Is that I e'er from sin should cease;
Jesus, I look to Thy faithfulness;
If nothing is too hard for Thee,
All things are possible to me.

On the one hand, we must guard against putting anything beyond the
grace of God; even saying that God has never kept and never will keep a
redeemed person from sin. At the same time we must not tell others we
have reached a place of sinless perfection. All the resources of God are
available to us in this spiritual warfare; but our humanity is still the realm
of Satan's attack and on this level we remain susceptible to both
temptation and sin.

Our safety comes in our constant reliance upon the Holy Spirit, for in
Him we defeat temptation. In His power we triumph, and without Him we
will surely fall. Here is a suggestion which might help us grasp the
presence and work of the Holy Spirit in us. I have always wanted to be a
poet. I have even attempted to write a few poems, but in reading what I
have written, I must sadly conclude that I will never be a poet. But if
Shakespeare lived in me, what wonderful poetry I could write. I would
also enjoy being a composer, but I do not have that creative talent. But if
Beethoven lived in me, what music I could compose. I do want to live a
consistent Christian life and not give in to the tempter's suggestion to do
evil. But I cannot live a consistent Christian life; I am too human and
sinful. But if Christ lived in me, what a wonderful life I could live.
Shakespeare will never live in me and so I will never be a poet.
Beethoven will never live in me and so I will never be a composer. But I
can have Christ live in me and so I can live a consistent Christian life.

Even though this perfect Christ lives in us, we are imperfect people; we still sin. But we need not turn completely away from Christ. Rather we can go to our Advocate, our blessed Lord, repent of the sin, and find forgiveness. Then we can forgive ourselves and move from that point of failure to serve the Lord with joy.

LIFE RESPONSES

1. Do you think it is possible for a born-again person to sin? Doesn't the book of John declare that "He who is born of God does not sin?"

2. What does it mean when we declare "we are saved from the practice of sin?"

3. Do Wesleyans define sin adequately or do you prefer the Calvinist concept of sin? What are the weaknesses of each definition?

4. What traps should we avoid if we are overtaken in a sin? Which trap was most tempting to you?

5. How is it possible to make too much of the sin committed by a believer?

6. How does the Holy Spirit in our lives assist us in living a life free of the practice of sin?

12

HOW WILL IT ALL
END/BEGIN?

A fter Jesus had returned to heaven, an angel told His disciples that *"This same Jesus, who has been taken from you into heaven, will come back in the same way you have seen him go into heaven"* (Acts 1:11). That announcement, along with other promises in the gospels and the epistles, has led to the Christian belief that Jesus will return again physically, will be with His people, and will rule over them. The personal second coming of Jesus Christ is at the very heart of biblical redemptive truth. We have already been saved from the guilt of sin and delivered from its power; but our redemption will not be complete until Christ returns and we are delivered from the very physical effects of sin.

God's redemptive purpose involves not only the salvation of individuals, but also of human society. The Bible teaches that the power and reign of Satan manifests itself not only in the sin, the physical sufferings, and the mortality of individuals, but also in the evils of all historical experience. God is sovereign, and Satan can do nothing apart from His will; yet God has permitted Satan to exercise his power over human history. Every generation, and certainly this present one, has witnessed diabolical evils which we would think impossible for enlightened, civilized people. And it seems that the demonic element in history is increasing.

God will not allow Satan to exercise his power in human history forever, though. Humankind will not obliterate itself, nor will this planet become a cold, lifeless star. There will come a day when the knowledge of God will cover the earth as the waters cover the sea, and peace and righteousness will prevail instead of war and evil. When God one day takes the reins of government into His hands, the kingdom of God will come to earth and His will be done even as it is done in heaven. Then He will be King of Kings and Lord of Lords. The second coming of Christ is an indispensable doctrine in the biblical teaching of our redemption. If not for His glorious return, God's work would forever be incomplete. Christ on the cross is the center of redemption past. Christ returning in glory is the center of redemption future.

Most of the information about Christ's return is given in the book of Revelation. However, Revelation does not mention every detail and is highly symbolic. So while there has been almost universal agreement in the Church that Christ is returning, there has been no such agreement on the time and circumstances of His coming. Unfortunately, this has created serious divisions among Christians and, at times, great bitterness. Perhaps this is why some preachers and teachers are hesitant to address the subject at all. That is unfortunate and unsound, for the Bible has many verses, paragraphs, and parables from our Lord which center on His second coming. To refuse to preach or discuss such an important subject simply because it is irritating to some, is to be untrue to the Bible message. So I move forward knowing that many pieces of the time and circumstances of Christ's return are at present unknown or misunderstood.

> *God will not allow Satan to exercise his power in human history forever, though. Humankind will not obliterate itself, nor will this planet become a cold, lifeless star.*

Before discussing the predominant interpretations of Christ's return, I will briefly point out four elements described in Revelation.

1) The evil which has marked human history will, at the end of the age, be incarnated into a "superman" called the Antichrist, who will rule the world and achieve a union of church and

state so that people will be forced to worship him or suffer economic sanctions and death.

2) This Antichrist, empowered by Satan, will direct his hostility toward God and the people of God. During his reign, God's people will suffer the most terrible persecution history has ever witnessed. This time of suffering is called the "Great Tribulation." It will last seven years until, at last, God's divine wrath will pour out on the Antichrist and those who worship him.

> *Premillennialists believe that the reference in Revelation 20 to the thousand years of peace is a literal or at least a fixed period of time that follows the triumphant return of Christ.*

3) Another very important element in these end times is God's treatment of the Jewish people. The veil will be taken from their minds, and they will turn as a people in faith to Jesus as their Messiah. They will refuse to worship the Antichrist and will suffer a fearful martyrdom.

4) The Antichrist will prevail temporarily, but his reign will be brief. At some point, Christ will visibly return in power and glory to punish the Antichrist along with those who have worshipped him; He will deliver His people from the tribulation, and establish a kingdom of peace on the earth that lasts for one thousand years.

According to this brief outline of prophetic teaching, the kingdom of God will not fully come until Jesus returns in glory. The second coming of Christ is the hope of the Church and the hope of human history. His coming will mean salvation and justice. Although this teaching is widely held throughout most of the Christian church, there are three main positions regarding the timing of Christ's return in the end times.

THE PREMILLENNIAL VIEW

Premillennialists believe that the reference in Revelation 20 to the thousand years of peace is a literal or at least a fixed period of time that follows the triumphant return of Christ. Since the return of Christ seems to be described in Scripture as imminent—that is, He could return at any time—He must be coming before the millennium.

Premillennialists observe that while the world seems to be getting better in some aspects (pointing to the arrival of the millennium), it is getting worse in many other aspects. That is, the very discoveries which seem to bring progress usually have within them the seeds of their own destruction and decay. We invent planes to transport us around the world quickly. But planes that carry medicine to the needy in remote places are the same planes that can drop the hydrogen bomb, killing those we may have been so anxious to help. We eliminated polio and with equal ingenuity have learned how to destroy in mass the very children the polio vaccine saved. Indeed, evil is so entrenched in the very matrix of society, that only the Lordship of Christ returning in power seems equal to the task of turning the world around.

One of the greatest controversies within premillennialism is in determining when the Church will be taken up with Christ, or raptured. Revelation reveals that there is a time of tribulation before the millennium, but will the believers be raptured before, during, or after the Tribulation? This is a touchy subject because whether we as Christians must go through the Tribulation depends on that timing. And in trying to rearrange the Scriptures to figure out the timing of the rapture, a whole Pandora's box of endless speculation and argument is opened up.

Pre-tribulationism. A narrow interpretation of the meaning of *imminence* in relation to Christ's return has many people believing that a rapture of the church will happen before the Tribulation. If by *imminence* we mean that there is no prophesied event that must yet take place before Christ raptures the Church, then it seems logical that this could happen at any time and will do so before the Tribulation.

The teaching of a pre-tribulation rapture has been widely circulated in North America. Strong Calvinists usually adopt this view and, interestingly enough, many other Evangelicals have come to believe that this view must be accepted or else one is a heretic of sorts. Even in churches like The Wesleyan Church, the pre-tribulation view of premillennialism has become so entrenched, that to preach another view of premillennialism sometimes brings sharp criticism and serious questioning of that person's true beliefs. This is tragic indeed.

It was not until the nineteenth century that pre-tribulationism gained popularity, particularly through the teachings of J. N. Darby, a Plymouth Brethren minister. In our day, the pre-tribulation rapture view is taught by

Hal Lindsey and other such writers. Pre-tribulationism is so popular because it believes that the Church is raptured out of the world before the Tribulation begins. This is certainly a great source of comfort for, after all, who wants to go through such hardship? To look forward to the second coming of Christ as our final hope and redemption as the Church does, and yet to teach that the Church must endure the terrible experiences of those awful days seems to rob His return of its blessedness. The real question, though, is not what we want to believe, but what does the Bible teach? Although this is an extremely appealing argument for Christ's return, does it agree with the Word of God? No theology can rest finally on what is

> *It was not until the nineteenth century that pre-tribulationism gained popularity, particularly through the teachings of J. N. Darby, a Plymouth Brethren minister.*

appealing or not appealing. Unfortunately, most of the books and religious magazines which speak of the "end times" take the pre-tribulationist view. The result is that many assume that conservative theology must include the teaching of the rapture of the Church before the Tribulation.

My intention is to give an overview of the beliefs about the time schedule of our Lord's return and not to prove or disprove any particular theory. Years of study on this subject, however, make me less and less comfortable with the teaching of the pre-tribulation rapture of the Church. The major flaw is that pre-tribulationists essentially say that Christ will return twice, although they would not describe it that way. The first is when Christ returns secretly to rapture His church before the Tribulation, and the second when He returns fully revealed to establish His millennium kingdom. I would like very much for the pre-tribulationists to be correct, but I fail to find strong scriptural support for this theory. In addition, while I have found references in the early Christian fathers that support the imminence of Christ's return, I do not find that any of them taught a pre-tribulation rapture.

The Didache—dating back to the first quarter of the second century—is one of the earliest pieces of Christian literature after the New Testament. *The Didache* encourages a spirit of expectancy and watchfulness in view of the uncertainty of the time of Christ's return. At the same time, the author expects the Church to suffer at the hands of the

Antichrist during the Tribulation, and he expects the coming of Christ to occur only at the end of this time of trouble.

> There shall appear the deceiver of the world as a Son of God, and shall do signs and wonders and the earth shall be given over into his hands and he shall commit iniquities which have never been seen since the world began. Then shall the creation of all mankind come to the fiery trial and many shall be offended and be lost, but they who endure in their faith shall be saved by the curse itself. And then shall appear the signs of the truth. First the sign spread out in heaven, then the sign of the trumpet, thirdly the resurrection of the dead; but not all the dead, but as it was said, The Lord shall come and all His saints with Him. Then shall the world see the Lord coming on the clouds of Heaven.

It is after the Tribulation, according to *The Didache*, that signs of the end shall appear, the final sign being the resurrection of the righteous. Then at last the Lord will come with His saints who have died. The purpose of the Didachist in writing this exhortation was to prepare the Church for the Tribulation and the sufferings that shall be inflicted by the Antichrist.

> *It is after the Tribulation, according to The Didache, that signs of the end shall appear, the final sign being the resurrection of the righteous. Then at last the Lord will come with His saints who have died.*

Mid-tribulationism. In the premillennial camp are also those who believe that Christ will return at the mid-point of the Tribulation to rapture His saints. During the final three and a half years of the Tribulation, the Antichrist will be discovered for what he really is. I do not develop this view further since it is burdened with the same difficulties of the pre-tribulation position in teaching two comings of the Lord—the first in the rapture during the Tribulation and the second before the millennium.

Post-tribulationism. Those who teach a post-tribulation rapture believe both the rapture of the Church and Christ's return in power are one event. At the end of the Tribulation, which the Church will endure, Christ will return and rapture His believers. These raptured believers will meet with Christ and those who have died earlier and come back to earth where Christ will establish the millennial kingdom.

Post-tribulationists have trouble with those Scriptures that seem to indicate that Christ's return is imminent because there are prophecies which, it appears, need to be fulfilled before the second coming of our Lord—primarily the Tribulation itself. The post-tribulationalists meet this difficulty by pointing out that the Bible does not use the words *imminent* and *watch*—on which the pre-tribulationists largely base their teaching of the imminent return of Christ—to refer to the second coming of Christ. The use of *watch* in Mark 13:33 and in Luke 21:36 refers to events that take place during the latter part of the Tribulation rather than to a secret coming of Christ. Obviously this debate will only be answered when Christ actually does return.

THE POSTMILLENNIAL VIEW

Postmillennialists believe that Christ will return after the Church has ushered in the millennium of peace. These Christians emphasize social justice, the elimination of such evils as slavery, war, slums and disease, and encourage the sacrificial work of all Christians to bring the millennium to pass. They remind us that when Christ went away, the Holy Spirit came to be with us. Christ declared that the Holy Spirit would guide us and do great works through us. If indeed the Holy Spirit has the power to enlighten us and to do these things, then there is no reason why we should not continue to move toward a more perfect world in the millennium. After the millennium has run its course, Christ himself will return to judge and then to rule forever.

Postmillennialism was extremely popular in the early twentieth century. Modern science was making life so much better for everyone. And since World War I was the war to "end all wars," there would be peace, for modern man had at last learned the folly of bloodshed. Through education, science, political action, and the elimination of poverty, we would "learn war no more." Instead we would care for our neighbors around the world, a spirit of good will would prevail, and we would arrive at the point God intended all along. At long last the millennium would dawn. But it wasn't long after World War I that we began to suspect that paradise was not as close as we once thought. The events of the last half of the twentieth century, including World War II and the hydrogen bomb, have increased poverty, racial hatred, sexual perversion, crime, political corruption, the failure of popular religious leaders, and have made the postmillennialist extremely difficult to find.

> *Amillennialists see history as something that repeats itself over and over again as kingdoms rise and fall, and movements ebb and flow.*

The strength of the postmillennialists is that they take seriously the scriptural passage in Revelation 20 that introduces the concept of the millennium. They also are serious about the commands of Christ to feed the hungry, clothe the naked, and visit the imprisoned. They believe in the power of the Holy Spirit and that empowered and directed by Him, we can improve our world. Furthermore, they believe that the prophetic utterances about a great time of peace where the wolf and the lamb will lie down together refer to a good life right here on earth (Isaiah 11:6).

The postmillennialists have nothing, of course, to say about the imminence of Christ's return. It is simply not possible to observe what is happening in the world today and believe that Christ's return can happen at any given moment if you are a postmillennialist. To teach that Christ's return is imminent and that there is still time to correct all the evils of the world before He returns are not compatible views.

THE AMILLENNIAL VIEW

Since the millennium is only mentioned once in the Bible, and that in the book of Revelation where much of the language is poetic and figurative and where numbers are subject to all kinds of interpretations, amillennialists bypass the idea of the millennium and proceed to other matters.

Amillennialists see history as something that repeats itself over and over again as kingdoms rise and fall, and movements ebb and flow. It's a cycle rather than a progression toward greater evil as the premillennialists hold, or toward greater peace as the postmillennialists believe. At some point, the tension will be broken by a final apocalyptic event in history when Christ will return in the flesh; there will then be the final judgment and the new life which begins will be the eternal life promised to us.

Some amillennialists declare that if the millennium is real, then that period of time was ushered in already by Christ's first coming. Still other amillennialists would teach that the millennium is simply a description of that perfect life ushered in with Christ's return and which continues forever. The thousand years is simply figurative language suggesting the perfect and complete life of eternity.

The amillennial view is consistent to what we observe so frequently in our reading of history—the way apocalyptic judgments seem to fall on people, absorbing the impossible tensions of opposing forces, resolving events into a new synthesis, and giving humanity a fresh start. They believe that this process will move us eventually to the great event when history, as we know it, shall be finished. The amillennial view supports the imminence of Christ's return since we do not need to wait for life to reach the perfection of the millennium, as the postmillennialists believe, before Christ returns and rules with finality and power.

The flaw of the amillennialists is that they evade the millennium. They solve the problem of the millennium by eliminating it, simply allegorizing it out of existence. They see the solution of our problems in a day "beyond history." They do, however, insist on only one great Day of Judgment and so avoid many of the difficulties to which other interpreters of end-time events are subject.

IMPLICATIONS FOR EVANGELISM

I hope that at this point you don't decide that the whole subject of the second coming of Christ is too complicated, or too speculative, and therefore turn from it in impatience. Do remember that the people who study eschatology (the doctrine of end times) take what Scripture declares very seriously. In fact, people who are not Bible-believing Christians usually do not bother themselves about the subject at all. If those of us who discuss such topics are truly concerned about what the Scripture declares relative to the end of the age, we should find a way to keep from being too argumentative. Whatever position we may take, it is imperative that we keep the Bible as our only final authority. We should not be too dogmatic in the expression of our views, remembering that no person has the final, perfect word on this subject. There is just too much we do not fully understand.

A person's view of the second coming of Christ usually makes a difference, to some degree at least, in that person's approach to Christian service in general and evangelism in particular. Premillennialists, particularly pre-tribulation premillennialists, will probably be more interested in personal evangelism than in social reform. Since they believe that the time we have is brief, it is imperative to preach the gospel to as many people as possible before it is too late. However, the premillennialists will generally minimize social reform, not because they do not believe in it, but because first things must be put first. And the salvation of individuals comes before social reform.

The postmillennialists stress the social gospel. They believe in evangelism, of course, but they feel that we should have more compassion for people who need to be fed, clothed and housed. Did not Christ encourage us in this and even suggest that "if we do this for the least, we do it unto Him?" A passion for souls is important, the postmillennialist would argue, but don't forget compassion for the suffering. Certainly it is important to "get people ready to meet God," but these same people are starving to death, they are cold, hurting, and desperate. How can we neglect them in their obvious and urgent needs?

> *A person's view of the second coming of Christ usually makes a difference, to some degree at least, in that person's approach to Christian service in general and evangelism in particular.*

Amillennialists usually have strong convictions about election and predestination. "The times are in God's hands," they declare. We can evangelize individuals and we ought to; we can work for social reform and we ought to; and when the number of the chosen is filled, Christ will return. The amillennialists do evangelize and work for a better day, but they know that the millennium will not come because of their efforts, and that all people will not be saved despite their best efforts. Neither the perfect society nor the salvation of all people is within the eternal purposes of God. In any case, the amillennialists feel they are under orders to have passion and compassion. The issues finally are in God's hands; history will be fulfilled according to His plans, which are quite unknown to us.

WHAT DOES THE WESLEYAN CHURCH BELIEVE?

A person can be a premillennialist, a postmillennialist, or an amillennialist and be fully accepted in The Wesleyan Church. A person can hold that believers will be raptured by Christ preceding the Tribulation, or in the midpoint, or at the end of the Tribulation and still be in good standing with the Church. The Word of God simply does not speak clearly on the subject of the rapture of the Church. Wesleyans do believe in a personal and imminent return of Christ. We limit our pronouncement of end-time prophecy to that.

> *A person can be a premillennialist, a postmillennialist, or an amillennialist and be fully accepted in The Wesleyan Church.*

We do know this with certainty: 1) Christ will come again; 2) He will come again in a physical, visible, and powerful way; 3) He will come in judgment and in promise; and 4) no one knows when He will return, not even the angels—only the Father himself.

What we need to know is 1) are we looking for His return with anticipation? (2) Are we ready for His coming, having accepted forgiveness through His grace? (3) He is coming for His own; do we belong to Him?

LIFE RESPONSES

1. How many views are there about the millennium? Which one is most convincing to you? Explain.

2. Will Christ return before, in the middle of, or after the Great Tribulation in your judgment? Explain.

3. How has the pre-tribulation view affected the thinking of many Christians today regarding the end times? What is your opinion of this teaching?

4. Some Christian churches believe in amillennialism. How do you respond to this teaching?

5. Does one's view of the second coming of Christ impact evangelism? In what ways?

6. Are you prepared for Christ's return? If not, what steps should you take today to make preparation?

CONCLUSION

WHAT IS OUR
UNFINISHED TASK?

The Church has been put on earth to bring people to God so that they might know and walk with Him. The Church is a body of believers who enjoy fellowship with God, worship Him, and become Christ's Bride on earth, living in anticipation of complete, final, and perfect union with Him. But the Church has a job to do *now*—reaching the masses beyond their doors who still do not know God.

Evangelism is the Christian's primary work and, with discipleship, our most important work. The Lord's Prayer begins with the petition *"Hallowed be Thy Name."* It is the prayer that Christ taught us to pray . . . that first and foremost God's Name is to be hallowed throughout the earth. His Name is not honored by people who do not know Him as their Father and Redeemer. Our task is to bring everyone to that place where they know Him as such and honor His name in their lives. That is evangelism. Teaching people who know Christ to honor God's name better is discipleship. The two tasks must always stand side by side. The degree to which we sense this responsibility and the means by which we fulfill that duty will be determined, in part, by our belief system relative to the theological issues raised in previous chapters.

Roman Catholicism views evangelism as uniting people to Christ through the Catholic Church and its sacraments. The Vatican Council declared that "God has instituted the Church through His only-begotten Son, and has bestowed on it manifest marks of that institution, that it may be recognized by all men as the guardian and teacher of the revealed Word of God; for to the Catholic Church alone belong all those admirable tokens which have been established for the evident credibility of the Christian faith." The Catholic Church sees a person receiving salvation through the sacrament of baptism within the Catholic system.

> *Our task is to bring everyone to that place where they know Him as such and honor His name in their lives. That is evangelism.*

John Calvin reacted strongly against the limited access to God and salvation taught by the Catholic Church and then developed a system of salvation, a system with its own limitations. Believing as he did that new birth precedes faith (a person believes in Christ because God saved him rather than a person receiving salvation because he believes), Calvin faced a difficult dilemma regarding evangelism . . . how to promote missionary and evangelistic work and remain true to his fundamental teachings. When William Carey felt called to leave England and go to India, his mission board made a comment that summarized the Calvinist system: "If God wanted the heathen of India saved, he could save them without William Carey." Evangelism and missionary work contradict the belief that Jesus did not die for all. Fortunately, like many Catholics, many Calvinists depart from their strict theology far enough to respond with their hearts to the lost of this world.

However, all those, including Wesleyans, who teach that Christ died for all and that every person has a choice to believe in Christ, see evangelism as their first duty—to enable people to hear the Word of the Lord, that they might respond to the preceding grace which ultimately will lead to their salvation.

WHAT IS EVANGELISM?

Evangelism is specific: God wants His children to present Jesus Christ to the world in the power of the Holy Spirit so that people will trust God through Him, accept Him as their Savior, and serve Him as their Lord in the fellowship of His Church. Living a good Christian life is not evangelism—it is pre-evangelism. Such a life produces admiring observers and helps people be receptive to the Word of God. But Christianity cannot be radiated. It is not only an attitude and a spirit, but a body of truth about God and His Son that must be accepted. Knowledge of this truth can no more be radiated than knowledge of arithmetic. Evangelism must be definite and confrontational. By that I do not mean anything negative, but rather tenderly bringing people face-to-face with the claims of Christ.

Evangelism is more than being a witness. The witness of the Church in life and ministry is vital, but it alone is not evangelism. The Church must literally "go out after people." It has been said that if a man builds a better mousetrap, the world will beat a path to his door. But this was never true of mousetraps and it is not true of churches. A church's good influence in a community may produce well-disposed outsiders who will remain outsiders until someone says to each individual, "This is for you."

Oscar Wilde once wrote of his Aunt Jane who died of mortification because no one came to her grand ball. She died without knowing that she had failed to mail out the invitations. That is the story of many churches that have wonderful worship services, splendid programs, and everything except a way of making some connection with those outside—those who always assume that the church is for someone else.

> *Living a good Christian life is not evangelism—it is pre-evangelism.*

Evangelism is not feeding the hungry, or going to a board retreat or a married couples encounter. It is not a catchword for ornamentation. Evangelism must be saved from these generalities and be employed for something very specific—bringing people to faith in Christ.

THE WHY OF EVANGELISM

God is love and love cannot exist in loneliness. God created human beings to have fellowship with Him and to enjoy His blessings. Apart from Him, people are off-center. As St. Augustine put it, "God has made us for Himself so that our hearts are restless until they find their rest in Him."

> *"The Gospel is true always and everywhere or it is not a Gospel at all." William Temple*

God has put some knowledge of Himself in every person. *"He left not Himself without witness"* (Acts 14:17 KJV). There is a law, according to Paul in Romans, written on every person's heart. But it is still a leap to enter God's presence and the life he has provided through His Son Jesus Christ. Those who have not found this life, which Christ alone makes possible, are living without ever knowing why they were born. They are missing the greatest good that life can have. If we believe that we are living among those who are missing so much, then all our love and pity should drive us with desperate urgency to do something about it. Christians who have experienced how much difference Christ makes cannot help but feel passionate sympathy for those who have not. That is the motive for evangelism which has carried the gospel over the oceans and mountains and centuries—all the way to us.

William Temple, the Archbishop of Canterbury early last century, said, "The Gospel is true always and everywhere or it is not a Gospel at all." There is no one we are not supposed to win; the Christian life is for everyone on earth. We are all born with the capacity and the need to come to God through Jesus Christ.

Furthermore, if it hurts us to see people without the hope of Christ, think how it hurts Him. The Cross is our clue. It was for our neighbors that Jesus died. He himself is the shepherd in the parable who could not rest as long as one sheep was missing from the fold. The one commandment which Jesus repeated in all of His final meetings with His disciples was the commandment to go out and tell others about himself. We are His channels of salvation, the instruments of His love. If we fail, to that extent, *"the cross of Christ be emptied of its power"* (1 Corinthians 1:17).

THE GOAL OF EVANGELISM

Christianity is not a creed or a ritual of ethics . . . but a personal relationship with Jesus Christ. Evangelism must bring people to the experience of God's presence so they will begin each day with a sense of partnership with Him and go to sleep each night secure in the knowledge of His love. Unfortunately, many people accept the truth about God intellectually without ever coming to God himself. We may be like the geese in Kierkegaard's parable who regularly assembled to praise the glories of the wide, soaring flights—though they themselves never left the barnyard. Evangelism must help people not only to know about God, but also to know Him.

In addition to introducing people to Christ, evangelism also helps people to know and understand what they believe. A Christian must believe that there is a God and that He is good and powerful; that Jesus Christ is God and came to this earth as our Savior from sin; and that Christ is alive, a living Friend and Lord. People need to believe these things, not just give assent to the words. If they don't know what these words mean, they may think becoming a Christian signifies only that they want to be decent or do not want to be heathen.

Immanuel Kant said, "Every personality is like a pyramid resting on its apex." He meant that there is one basic choice which influences every other choice in life. That basic choice at the point of the pyramid is to have faith. This choice determines our goals, our priorities, and our destiny. Paul said that when this key choice is changed to faith in Christ, a person becomes a "new creature." This is God's desire for every person.

> *We need to always remember that it is unnatural to live apart from God. It is a distortion of nature.*

THE WHO OF EVANGELISM

The basic assumption of evangelism is always this: we are created to be Christians; it is abnormal to be away from Christ. We need to always remember that it is unnatural to live apart from God. It is a distortion of nature. Knowing Christ restores our personalities.

Some people have a deep sense of guilt from which they are longing to be free, but more likely, they believe they are doing as well as can be expected. Evangelism not only brings the good news of salvation but often must enforce the bad news that people are lost. The message doesn't change, but we must state the gospel so that people outside the Church will connect it with their needs and desires. People do feel something is missing. They want to sense a reality beyond this world. The Church can bring something no secular institution can, something beyond this world.

> *If people can see more of Christ, they will grow in their appreciation of Him until they are ready to give Him not only their admiration, but also their lives.*

Christ himself is by far the most effective means of evangelism, for He is the message. Many who criticize the Church and Christians will not criticize Christ. They love and admire Him. The Russian author Fyodor Dostoyevsky once wrote to his brother, "I want to say to you that I am a child of this age, a child of unbelief and skepticism. And yet . . . I believe there is nothing lovelier, deeper, more sympathetic, more rational, more human, and more perfect than the Savior." Evangelism should start at that point. If people can see more of Christ, they will grow in their appreciation of Him until they are ready to give Him not only their admiration, but also their lives. If Christ is lifted up, He will draw all people to Him. We may not understand how this works, but the fact is that Christ, because of His atoning death, is able to draw people from their evil habits, from their lesser loyalties, and enable them to give their hearts to Him.

The task is indeed unfinished. But we may still be at the beginning of the Christian era. The distance separating us from the Cross and the Resurrection is only a hand's breadth of time. If the influence of Jesus has penetrated so deeply in the brief span of two thousand years, what might be its impact in two million? That may be a fanciful thought, I know, but who can tell the length of God's time of grace?

I must admit that this is a fearful world if we see only the human factors. There is no hope for history there, but ample grounds for fatalism and despair. We must recognize another factor though, the dimension of the supernatural. Ours is essentially an incarnational faith, and when *"the Word became flesh,"* it was a declaration that the supernatural is deeply concerned with the material, temporal world (John 1:14a). Fortunately for us, God does not stand outside the historical process, but has involved himself in it. There is a love that will not let history go; there is a Spirit who still moves upon the face of the waters; there is a long-suffering Lord who comes with salvation yet today.

OUR BASIS OF HOPE

The work of God in the world is not finished. It was not to desert history that Christ returned to the Father, but to bind history to himself forever. The Christian will not despair until the Lord God has abdicated His throne or Christ confesses that His passion was a blunder and the truth for which He died a lie. God in Christ is still working out His purpose through the Holy Spirit, and human calculations cannot assess the operations of the Spirit.

Christ won a decisive victory on the cross and with His resurrection. And so we are facing a defeated enemy as we assault the darkness of the world. The worst is past. The outcome of the conflict can never be in doubt. The cosmic battle between truth and error will never tremble again in the balance. Christ will never again die on Calvary. *"Since Christ,"* says the Word of God, *"was raised from the dead, he cannot die again"* (Romans 6:9). *"It is finished,"* (John 19:30) was His cry on the cross.

We must not close our eyes to the reality of the present. There will be yet a great deal of toil and tears. There is, however, a wonderful fact that God is reconciling the world to himself in Christ. That divine deed accomplished on a hill outside Jerusalem towers forever over the struggle of the ages. The Bible knows nothing of that uneasy dualism of the Greeks, as though the Kingdom of God and the empire of evil were locked together in a perpetually indefinite and indecisive struggle. The initiative belongs to God. This is His world, not Satan's. When it seems everything has gone wrong and the brief triumphs of evil seem to frustrate God's purposes, remember that nothing can ultimately defeat His will.

We do not know when it all shall end or precisely how. But our task right now is to be Christ's witness throughout the entire earth. And it is not too much to hope that such obedience to the Great Commission may not only make some crooked places straight and some rough places plain, but actually speed the Lord's return and hasten the final appearing. So be it. Even so come Lord Jesus.

LIFE RESPONSES

1. How does our theology of salvation influence our evangelistic efforts?

2. Do you agree that "lifestyle evangelism" is really just pre-evangelism and that we must be more confrontational? Why?

3. In what ways should we be more confrontational?

4. If Christ is the most effective means of evangelism, how do we lift Him up without getting in the way?